THE K   OF TIME

THE RULE OF TIME

A Different Look at the Values of
Time by Said Nursi

Yunus Çengel

NEW JERSEY • LONDON • FRANKFURT • CAIRO

TUGHRA
BOOKS
New Jersey

Published by Tughra Books
335 Clifton Avenue, Clifton
New Jersey 07011, USA

www.tughrabooks.com

Library of Congress Cataloging-in-Publication Data

Names: Çengel, Yunus A., author.
Title: The rule of time : a different look at the values of time by Said Nursi / Yunus Çengel.
Other titles: Zamanın hükmü. English
Description: New Jersey : Tughra Books, [2016] | Includes bibliographical references. | Translated from Turkish.
Identifiers: LCCN 2015045988 | ISBN 9781597843966 (alk. paper)
Subjects: LCSH: Time--Religious aspects--Islam. | Nursi, Said, 1873-1960--Philosophy. | Nurculuk.
Classification: LCC BP190.5.T54 C4613 2016 | DDC 297.8/3--dc23
LC record available at http://lccn.loc.gov/2015045988

ISBN: 978-1-59784-396-6

Printed by
Çağlayan A.Ş., Izmir - Turkey

Contents

As my biography which you have in your hands proves, I was a religious republican before any of you, with the exception of the Chairman of the Court, was born. A summary is this: like now, I was living at that time in seclusion in a remote tomb. They used to bring me soup, and I would give breadcrumbs to the ants. I used to eat my bread, having dipped it in the soup. They asked me about it and I told them: The ant and bee nations are republicans. I give the breadcrumbs to the ants out of respect for their republicanism.

Then they said to me: "You are opposing the righteous early generations of Islam." I told them in reply: "The four Rightly-Guided Caliphs were both Caliphs and Presidents of the Republic. Abu Bakr the Veracious, may God be pleased with him, the Ten Promised Paradise, and the Companions of the Prophet were like presidents of the republic. But not as an empty name and title, they were heads of a religious republic which bore the meaning of true justice and freedom in accordance with the Sharia."

Bediüzzaman Said Nursi's answer to the question, "What do you think of the republic?" during his defense in Afyon Court in 1949.

Who Is Bediüzzaman Said Nursi?[1]

B ediüzzaman Said Nursi was born in the village of Nurs, Bitlis, Hizan in 1876. He had an innovative, daring, and brave character, very brilliant intelligence and a strong memory. When they united with absolute belief and love of knowledge, he completed the classical madrasah education, which normally lasted fifteen years, in three months. He proved himself by winning debates organized by those who could not accept this extraordinary development. Therefore, Said Nursi, who had been known as "Mullah Said," was given the title "Bediüzzaman," which means "the unique being of time."

Bediüzzaman, who dealt with the problems of the community he lived in along with the common problems of humanity, observed the following: The West got stuck in materialism and the East could not form a structure based on belief by renewing its institutions that grew old. The Ottoman State had the same problem. The state and the nation were subject to Islam in appearance, but they broke away from Islam spiritually. They did not fully understand the change in the West and the structure of this change.

According to Bediüzzaman, monarchy prevented all kinds of development and it was necessary to move to constitutional monarchy based on consultation. To this end, it was necessary to struggle against "the three great enemies": ignorance, poverty, and conflict. He developed a project of education to do it. According to this project, educational insti-

---

[1] This part was compiled from various resources. Detailed information can be obtained from www.bediuzzaman.net, www.nursistudies.com, www.risalaera.com and many other websites.

tutions called "Madrasatuzzahra" would be established all over the country; they would have elementary, junior high, and senior high schools; religious subjects along with exact sciences would be taught there.

He went to Istanbul in 1907 to present his views to the Sultan. However, Istanbul, the capital city of the empire, had been corrupted together with the empire. When the views he uttered in Istanbul harassed the palace, he was sent to a mental hospital. However, the doctors at the mental hospital wrote a report stating that he was sane. Bediüzzaman did not have difficulty in making himself accepted among the famous scholars of Istanbul after the scholars of the east. Those who talked to him received answers to their most complicated questions and could not help saying, "You are really Bediüzzaman." His views on freedom, which based constitutional monarchy on Islamic principles, attracted great attention.

During the First World War, he established a militia regiment from his volunteer students. During Bitlis Defense, he was injured and was captured by Russians. After living in captivity for about three years, he escaped. After he returned from captivity, he became a member of "Daru'l-Hikmati'l-Islamiyya," the only Islamic Academy of that period, as the candidate of the army.

Against the fatwa declaring the national struggle in Anatolia a revolt, he issued a counter fatwa together with the scholars of Anatolia. Due to a book he published against the British invaders during the invasion of Istanbul, he was sentenced to death in absentia by the invaders. Due to these activities, he was invited to the Grand National Assembly in Ankara in 1922. They held an official welcoming ceremony for him at the Assembly. However, when he saw that a very serious difference of direction was about to form between the new administrators and the nation, he issued a declaration containing ten articles and distributed it in the Assembly. Then, he returned to Van.

Although Bediüzzaman had no connection with the incident of Sheikh Said, and he always opposed all kinds of revolt by saying, "Swords cannot be used against the members of this nation," he was sent into exile like many oppressed people. He was sent into exile to Burdur and then to Barla. He started to write the *Risale-i Nur* in Barla and he virtually became a school on his own.

Bediüzzaman Said Nursi developed a style to explain the principles that formed the foundations of Islam with his work called *Risale-i Nur* against the policies to inactivate religion in Turkey in 1925. With the style he developed, Bediüzzaman explained the truths of belief by combining the mind, heart, and feelings. Thus, he presented a brand-new viewpoint by combining *Kalam*, Sufism and positive sciences; he eliminated the discrimination between schools and dervish lodges.

Bediüzzaman was arrested due to these efforts several times, and was sent to prison in Eskişehir (1935), Denizli (1943) and Afyon (1947). Although he was acquitted of any wrongdoing, he was always under prosecution.

When Bediüzzaman died on March 23, 1960, in Urfa, the material possessions he left as inheritance were a teapot, a few glasses, an old shirt, a patched gown, a turban, a *siwak*, ten lira, a little tea and sugar. As spiritual inheritance, he left the *Risale-i Nur* Collection, which is a *tafsir* (interpretation) of the Qur'an in accordance with the understanding of the age, and which is based on four main books, namely, *Sözler* (The Words), *Mektubat* (The Letters), *Lem'alar* (The Gleams), and *Şualar* (The Rays).

Foreword

The age we live in is justifiably called the information age. Informatics and communication are the high values that set their stamps on our age. Informatics and communication technologies have surrounded the world like a net and penetrated into all segments of society. Those who see that the rising sun of science reach all sane people through the rays of communication, and that this enlightens the mind, will see that there is no place for ignorance and misunderstanding any longer. The world is entering a real process of enlightenment. In this modern age, in which knowledge doubles every five years, it is expected that no place will be left for ignorance and wrong knowledge to hide, and that the world will move speedily to brighter tomorrows. However, it looks as if enlightenment with true knowledge increases at the same time as blackening with wrong knowledge increases. Although it is expected that informatics and communication will increase mutual understanding and trust through correct knowledge, it can be seen that wrong knowledge and skepticism increase in the world and conflicts soar. The biggest threat to world peace and the future in this age of enlightenment is wrong knowledge, which is the worst form of ignorance, and the groundless suspicions originating from this wrong knowledge. The most efficient struggle against this threat can be carried out by being equipped with correct knowledge and avoiding acts that cause suspicion.

A strange situation in this age of intellect and science is that there is still a contradiction in terms; hence, opposites are confused; slavery to desires is thought of as freedom; laicism, which necessitates treating religiousness and irreligiousness equally, is confused with enmity to religion; some prejudices and fixed ideas are presented as science; many people who are ahead of their time are called reactionists, while some people who cannot stand democracy act as if they are advocates of democracy.

In modern Turkey, one of the primary people who is widely known to be opposite to what they in fact represented is probably Bediüzzaman Said Nursi. Although he was acquitted of all charges against him and half a century has passed after his death, very few people are familiar with Bediüzzaman's views, especially regarding modern concepts like freedom, republic, democracy, and laicism. When his work, the *Risale-i Nur* Collection, is studied carefully, it is clear that Bediüzzaman is very religious, but also a strong advocate of freedom, republicanism, democracy, freedom of religion and conscience.

Nursi has very clear views regarding terror and globalization. He emphasized the decree of the Qur'an regarding killing an innocent person to be equal to killing the whole population of the world; he regarded punishing others due to the mistake of another person as cruelty and oppression. He stated one century ago that struggles would no longer be through the sword but instead through the pen. He saw that the world was on its way to being a single village through globalization; instead of struggling against this reality, he put forward the principles of globalization and tried to streamline this current. Nursi is an exceptional person who reconciled piety and religiousness with a high level of intellect, logic, and reasoning within the framework of the realities of his time and by the confirmation of conscience.

Introduction

H umanity goes through different phases of growth, just like individuals do, and progresses toward maturity. This progression, which started with savagery and continued with slavery, has settled in this age on individual rights and freedoms that put the individual at the center stage of justice. The prominent feature of this modern age of liberty is that freedom is the rule and any prohibition is the exception. Governments have been restructured to establish true justice and to uphold individual rights and freedoms in the broadest possible way, and the political systems have been transformed into democracies in which the public opinion, which is a reflection of the public will, dominates. Change has always met with resistance, often led by conservative and religious entities. Bediüzzaman Said Nursi, a scholar of Islam and a philanthropic opinion leader, on the other hand, has been at the forefront of change in accordance with the rising values and realities of his time, instead of being in opposition. While his contemporaries opposed even positive reforms in the name of religion, Nursi applauded such reforms in the name of the very same religion, Islam, and showed that piety and some modern values did not contradict. Moreover, Nursi proved that Islam is the source of many modern values that are thought to contradict Islam.

Waves of change come with their set of values beyond peoples' control, and these waves eradicate old values whose time has passed. Nursi correctly read the rising values of the time, and stood with the wind of change, rather than against it. He viewed efforts to carry the past into the future as asking for the impossible, and stated that those who row against the current will be swept away and go extinct. It will be seen in this book that Nursi, while a very pious man, is a strong advocate of freedom, republicanism, and democracy with the utmost respect for the freedom of faith and conscience, and that he reconciled these modern values, thought by some to contradict Islam, with Islam. He opposed all forms of despotism regardless of where it came from and whatever its name was. He supported every step taken toward freedom and democracy, such as the constitutional monarchy that is based on mutual consultation and peoples' participation in governance, and the declaration of the first constitution protecting individual rights and freedom in the last period of the Ottoman state. According to Nursi, Islam and despotism—a regime of prohibitions and oppression—are complete opposites of each other and can never be reconciled. Democracy is the most Islamic form of government, and it is more so in this age of freedom when public opinion rules. Nursi views the violation of the freedom of conscience and religion as an insult to humanity.

Nursi stated in his writings that he could live without bread but not without freedom, and portrayed freedom as the essence of the core of humanity. He views unlimited freedom as animalism and the captivity of one's desires, and draws the limiting line to freedom at 'harming neither oneself nor others.' He defined constitutional monarchy, and later republicanism, as the sovereignty of the people, and characterized himself from an early age as a pious republican. He states that the Rightly Guided Four Caliphs, who were elected by the first Muslim community by their free will, were presidents in a true sense. He points to this application in the earliest and purest stage of Islam, and the verses from the Qur'an instructing consultation, as proofs that republicanism is the form of administration most suitable to Islam. Nursi states that the time of the regimes based on the ruling of a single authority—monarchy, sultanate, caliphate—has passed. He expresses that now is the time for governance for both religious and state entities via an assembly that represents public opinion and conducts affairs on the basis of consultation and sciences. Nursi views all forms of headship, including the presidency, as servanthood, and he bases this view on a hadith that says, "The chief of a society is the one who serves its people," which he labeled as a constitution of Islam. He also bases the freedom of conscience, which forms the foundation of correctly implemented secular systems as well as democracy, on this fundamental principle of Islam, and regards democracy and freedom of conscience among basic rights and freedoms. Nursi defines republicanism as a system of justice, mutual consultation, and the power bestowed only in the law, and claims that the fundamental principles of republicanism can be extracted from Islam. Therefore, he states, there can be no conflict between republicanism and Islam so long as justice is taken as the basis.

Nursi has always approached events as a true realist. He read the changing times and the changing conditions correctly, and he based his moves not on delusion, but on real time and space. In his interpretation of the Qur'anic verse, "there is no compulsion in religion," Nursi states that the freedom of conscience is a basic right and freedom for the people of our time, and that it will be implemented as a constitutional principle and a political criterion worldwide. Nursi did not regard non-Muslims acting as administrators in a Muslim country as objectionable.

Nursi explains that 99 percent of sharia is concerned with morality, worship, the afterlife, and virtue, which fall under the freedom of conscience and have no connection to state affairs or politics. He relegates the remaining 1 percent dealing with state affairs and politics to understanding politicians. Nursi rejects any notion claiming that constitutionalism or republicanism is contrary to sharia, and asserts that the essence of republicanism comes from sharia. He expresses that in sharia, general societal agreement constitutes a valid base, public opinion forms a foundation, and the general public tendencies are a valid criteria in decision-making. He states that in a properly functioning democracy, a parliament comprising of three hundred members can reach agreement only on what is good and beneficial for the society. And that such decision-making is in perfect conformity with sharia. Therefore, it can be said that the regimes that are based on reason, science, and consultation within the framework of freedom of speech and expression, and have the backing of the general public, are fully compatible with Islam together with the laws and regulations associated with the regimes so long as basic codes of morality such as justice and virtue are observed. This is because relying on reason, science, and public opinion in state government in these modern times is relying on Islam. Truths do not change by the change of their names.

According to Nursi, the most important matter for humanity is belief, and the greatest danger facing humankind is disbelief, which threatens eternal life. To him, gaining a strong belief is more important than gaining world dominion, and saving one's belief is like saving an eternal world. In his view, belief has the value of a diamond, while politics and worldly affairs are worth only pieces of glass, and thus using religion for political gain is a great injustice and insult to religion. If religion and politics are mixed in this time and age when all attention is turned to the world, and life in this world is given primary consideration, and life in the hereafter little consideration, it is unavoidable that politics will take center stage and religion will be pushed back to a supporting role. Politicization of religion is not a service to religion, which should be held above all worldly causes; rather, it is a disservice and even inflicts great harm and injustice on religion. Hence, Nursi stayed away from "political Islam" and promoted "civil Islam." He sought to win the hearts and minds via reason and convincing arguments and to turn peoples' attention to the hereafter from this world, rather than win influential governmental posts via politics. His goal was to save peoples' beliefs to secure eternal happiness rather than helping people gain temporary worldly benefit. That is, he used justice and observed balance in his approach to religion, and he did this on the basis of freedom of expression while staying within the limits of freedom of conscience, which is a modern value.

While technological innovations, progressing at a head-spinning pace, have made life easier and raised the quality of life to levels unimaginable half a century ago, the same technological innovations, when they fall into the wrong hands, can turn into dangerous devices that can destroy peace and order, and even threaten the very existence of humanity. The ease of destruction and the potential of technological wonders being used as weapons of terror have caused people concern and given them a gloomy outlook toward the future. Knowing that the existing amount of nuclear weapons have the power to destroy the entire world a hundred times over is causing us to question the future of humanity.

What's more, the ease of production and use of biological and chemical weapons of mass destruction that can destroy animals, plants, and innocent people have raised our level of concern. Transportation vehicles that are manufactured for peaceful purposes can turn an area into a war zone, and the military and security measures to prevent such use are proving to be inadequate.

No baby comes into this world as a terrorist, and no child dreams about becoming a terrorist when he or she grows up. Therefore, fighting terror is only possible by identifying and calming the feelings that move and feed the tendencies of destruction and hostility in people, who are at the highest level of creation. This can be made possible by Islam, which upholds justice, assistance, and love, and respects the rights of all creatures. The most effective war against terror can be fought by upholding 'righteousness' that establishes justice and peace, 'virtue' that results in brotherly love and harmony, and 'mutual assistance' that establishes unity and solidarity and eliminates fights. This can be made possible by equipping the current civilization that is based on force, benefit, and conflict with high moral values.

When the topic is terror and weapons of mass destruction, somehow Muslims come to peoples' minds first. This casts doubts on Islam, which is a religion of peace founded on love and a religion that equates the murder of one innocent person with the murder of humanity, and it also casts doubt on the religion's over a billion followers. The involvement of some people and states in terrorist acts with their Islamic identity, and their struggle to develop or possess weapons of mass destruction, also feed into these misconceptions. It should be declared from the highest positions of the Islamic world to the entire world with the loudest voice that: *"We as Muslims condemn the use of terror and weapons of mass destruction under all conditions; we view the murder of an innocent as the greatest cruelty and as a crime committed against humanity; and we consider those who attempt to use terror and weapons of mass destruction as the lowest and the cruelest of all people. We as Muslims are destroying all weapons of mass destruction—including nuclear weapons—in our possession, and we are terminating all research, development, and manufacturing activities of all such weapons. We also declare to the whole world that, even when we are bombarded with such weapons, we will never respond in kind."*

Such a call will have the effect of an atomic bomb in the minds of millions; it will shatter the thick walls of fear and prejudice built around Islam, and by removing the baseless fear and anxiety that are the only causes that can legitimize the use of weapons of mass destruction, it will serve as a virtual protective shield.

Being the inhabitants of the same globe, all people are naturally global. The advancements in transportation and communication technologies and the rise in the education level have pushed the limits of globalization further. Globalization has occurred to a large extent in sports, science, and even the economy. However, globalization that may be of great benefit to humankind also brings a lot of concerns with it. The main fear behind these concerns is the possibility that the strong will exploit the weak and even suppress them, and globalization will only benefit the wealthy. The best assurances against this danger are 'faith'; the sentiment that strength is in righteousness; and taking virtue, rather than benefit, as the base. This can only take place if the civilization that is based on material interests is educated by Islamic values.

In his *Risale-i Nur* collection, Nursi asserts that the foundations of positive globalization that will establish true peace on the globe and benefit both the rich and the poor are present in 'faith' that connects all humans and creation with the rope of brotherhood, and 'Islam' that does not neglect even the rights of an ant. The foundation of such a civilization is 'righteousness' that establishes justice and peace; its goal is 'virtue' that results in brotherly love and harmony, its fundamental principle is 'mutual assistance' that establishes unity and solidarity, and its result is 'happiness in this world and the hereafter.'

Some fundamental principles that Nursi emphasizes repeatedly are: the first step towards the betterment of social life is 'love and brotherhood'; the compassion that stems from true belief cannot allow aggression against the rights and freedoms of others; the true and lasting happiness of people is in 'virtue' that satisfies the high emotions and leads the spirit to sublime matters rather than material things; the bridge that provides order and accord in social life and establishes peace and tranquility among different social circles is '*zakah* (alms) and charity'; if this bridge is destroyed, instead of respect, obedience, and love from the poor to the wealthy, waves of rebellion, jealousy, and hatred will rise and destroy peace in humanity; it is only true justice that can prevent aggression and calm the conscience of people; no one should bear the burden of the crimes of others; the thing that is the most lovable is love, and the things that deserve animosity are animosity, enmity, and hatred; and affairs should be conducted with mutual consultation, which is the key to solidarity, progress, and happiness. Nursi's approach, which is based on reasoning with objective observation and logic, can be a source of inspiration for new initiatives regarding this issue and many other issues.

Chapter 1

Values of Time

Everything on earth has a certain life—even some truths that appear to be unchangeable. Every age comes with its own basket of values, and abolishes older values that have completed their time. Those who close their eyes to this reality and insist on doing business the old way are antiquated, and the result of this is backwardness and deviation from the contemporary world.

The majority of the truths are relative, not absolute—that is, they are based on time and space. When conditions change, many truths turn out to be wrong. For instance, water is always H2O and H2O is always water. However, water is in liquid form under certain circumstances; when the circumstances change, water becomes vapor or ice. Therefore, the discussion of whether water is liquid or solid is invalid. If the discussions had in order to find the truth generally end with differences of opinion, it is necessary to look for the reason in this detail, but it is not often heeded. This can only be possible when the debaters have true and comprehensive knowledge and sharp minds, when they free themselves from prejudice and obsession, and when they adopt a broad viewpoint. Zealous adherence to the truths that were once valid is a mark of ignorance, rote knowledge, and lack of reason and rationale. As Nursi puts it,

"Just as dress, food, and other medications need to change in the four seasons, so too the manner of education and upbringing of a person warrant changes in different stages of a person's life. Similarly, as necessitated by wisdom and need, religious provisions concerning secondary matters

*change in accordance with the stages of mankind's development. For very
many of these medicines were efficacious in mankind's infancy yet ceased
being remedies in youth. This is the reason the Qur'an abrogated some of its
secondary pronouncements. That is, it decreed that their time had finished
and that the turn had come for other decrees."*[2]

Similar things can be said about generalizations. For instance, if a
person tries to apply the following verse to everybody, he errs: *"Indeed,
mankind is very unjust, very ignorant"* (al-Ahzab 33:72). As Nursi puts
it, *"There are some verses and hadiths that are absolute (not have been
limited) but are regarded as general. There are also some that are valid
under certain conditions but are regarded as always valid. There are also
some that are conditional but are thought to be unconditional."*[3] That is,
some verses and hadiths are true in general but are regarded as applying
to anything; some belong to certain times but are regarded to be valid
any time; some are dependent on certain conditions but are regarded
as general.

When we look at the past, we see that there were some understandings that brought submissiveness and not using reasoning to the forefront, and regarded asking questions as irreligiousness. There were even
times when ignorance and bigotry were regarded as identical with religiousness. Even today, bigotry is regarded as a criterion for religiousness. However, Islam is not bigotry and it is contrary to ignorance. In the
world of exact sciences, bigotry and prejudice were presented under
the disguise of 'science.' However, science is not bigotry because these
kinds of mistakes are noticed and corrected by reasoning and investigative science in the course of time. Similarly, the way to find the essence
of the religion, to purify it from bigotry and prejudice that became part
of the religion over time, and to elevate the religion to the high position
it deserves in the modern world is to open the door of investigation
wide. The source of the religion is not the mind. However, a true religion does not contradict with a true mind and true science, because all
of them have the same source; there cannot be contradiction among
them. No religious decree can condemn the general mind and no reli-

---

[2]   *İşârâtü'l-İ'câz*, pp. 48–49.
[3]   *Sünûhât*, p. 12.

gious source can be explained in a way to exclude the mind. Not to be able to understand or to be too weak to understand is one thing, and to be contrary to ideas is something else.

Creation and Change

Movement and change are fundamental to the nature of creation, and from subatomic particles to galaxies, everything in the cosmos is in motion. Change brings about more freedom, and more freedom brings about more change. In the last century, the change in communities reached a head-spinning pace in parallel to the advancements in informatics and communication. The old world virtually goes and a new world virtually comes every ten years. That is, mini doomsdays strike all the time and a new system is established after each one. As Nursi puts it, *"We see that every century, indeed, every year and every season, one universe, one world, goes and another comes."*[4] The new universe comes with its own set of conditions, and its shell changes even though its kernel may remain the same. The engine of this change is freedom. It is not a coincidence that the countries that are the locomotive of the change and that determine its direction are the countries with the most freedom, and that the last wagon is full of the countries that are the most bigoted and prohibitive. There is a close relation between technological advancement, which is the driving force of change, and the environment of freedom; if one of them is missing somewhere, the other also disappears.

Perceiving the strong winds of change, Nursi regarded the desire to live in the new world by dreaming the old, and the efforts to carry the past into the future, as wishing for the impossible. And he took a firm stand: *"I will tell you a short word; you may memorize it. Here: the old way is no way; either new way or way to annihilation."*[5] That is, there are only two options: either to comply with the new conditions of the world and walk at the front lines with dignity, or to insist on keeping the

---

[4]   Nursi, B. S., *The Words*, The Thirty-Third Word, p. 716 (translation by Ş. Vahide), accessed September 29, 2014, www.dur.ac.uk/resources/sgia/imeis/words33_07_.pdf.
[5]   *Münâzarât*, p. 52.

old tradition and face humiliation and extinction. The direction and pace of the winds of change are beyond human control. Wise are those who move along with and not against these winds. Nursi states that those who move against the general current will eventually be wiped out and be annihilated: *"The general current will throw those moving in opposing direction into annihilation and nonexistence."*[6] Being such a realist and far-sighted person, Nursi should have been given the red-carpet treatment as a visionary. But instead, he was sent to mental institutions and prisons with charges of insanity and backwardness, and his fellow countrymen were condemned to poverty and humiliation. This is rather striking as it is indicative of the level of intellectual capacity of his contemporaries.

Nursi views the entire human race as a single human being, and attracts attention to the natural developmental stages of humankind from infancy to adulthood. This development process, which started with savagery and continued with slavery, has settled in this age on individual rights and freedoms that put the individual at the center: *"Looking from materialistic and historical perspectives, humankind has gone through several epochs. First came the savage and uncivilized era, second was the era of slavery, third was the era of captivity, fourth was the era of wages, and the fifth is the era of dominion and freedom."*[7]

That is, dominion and freedom in the broadest sense, which exhibits itself as public opinion and having a voice in governance, are the values marking the modern era we live in. Those who cannot grasp this and seek protection under the roof of prohibitions are the ones who are confined in the past. The appropriate thing for this age of liberty is for freedom to be the rule and any prohibition the exception.

The primary reasons behind divisions and clashing of ideas in the Islamic World are the examination and evaluation of issues from a narrow perspective, the disregard of the effects of changing times and conditions, and the inadequate involvement of mind and reason. However, as Nursi puts it in his book called *Münâzarât*, every time or age has

---

[6] *Muhâkemât*, p. 112.
[7] *Mektubat*, p. 353.

its own verdicts. If a person does not know the valid currency of his time and the direction that the course of time rows against the tide, his efforts will go down the drain. The general mind necessitates the elimination of some customs whose harms are more than their benefits and that are outdated. It is necessary to look at the possible consequences while evaluating events and ideas. What distinguish similar trees are their fruits.

Bediüzzaman Said Nursi mentions the importance of preserving the national values that connect individuals to one another in many places, but his main line is rationalism, not conservatism. As a matter of fact, he wants customs and traditions to be reviewed from time to time; he wants a comparison of benefits and harms of them to be made and the harmful ones to be removed. Those who are disturbed by this approach ask him, "Why do you despise our many deep-rooted customs?" He answers them as follows: "*Each time has a rule. The time we are in now decrees that some old customs be eliminated and abrogated. The superiority of their harms over their benefits justifies this elimination.*"[8] That is, the customs and traditions that bring more harm than benefits as the time and conditions change need to be buried in the graveyard of culture instead of kept. Nursi answers another question similarly: "*Time abrogates it. The superiority of its harms over its benefits justifies the elimination. It is not permissible to act upon abrogated rules.*"[9] He attracts attention to the probable results when evaluating events and ideas. That is, it is necessary to see what kind of fruits the seed of thought that is sown at the existing time and space will yield in the future: "*Look at the evidence and the consequences. . . . What distinguish alike trees are their fruits. Therefore, look at the consequences of my ideas and their ideas. In one it is rest and compliance. Hidden in the other are unrest and loss.*"[10] Or, in short, "*The thing that shows the essence of something is its fruit.*"[11]

This rationalist line away from emotionalism, sensitivity toward the values of time, the need and to filter everything through the mind

---

[8]   *Münâzarât*, p. 63.
[9]   Ibid., p. 76.
[10] Ibid., p. 50.
[11] *Muhâkemât*, p. 17.

outline Nursi's approach and view on events. He has his feet on the ground and does not confuse dream with truth: *"A single piece of truth is superior to a lot of dreams."*[12]

Rising Values: Mind, Science, Consultation

While interpreting verse 22 of the chapter of al-Baqarah in his work *İşârâtü'l-İ'câz* (Signs of Miraculousness), Nursi states: *"the source of Islam is knowledge (al-'ilm) and its base is reason or intellect (al-'aql)"*; and it is a necessity of Islam *"to accept the truth and reject fallacy and delusion."*[13] He often refers to Qur'anic phrases like *"So will they not reason,"* (Ya-Sin 36:68) *"So will they not think,"* (al-An'am 6:50) *"So will they not ponder on it,"* (an-Nisa 4:82) which have *"called on and encouraged reason and knowledge, and protected scholars."*[14] In the same work, he points out that Islamic principles and laws are established on rational proofs. Decisions related to secondary matters are left to the consultation of the minds to be derived from the original sources of the religion. This method of jurisprudence requires elaborating upon events and ideas in the light of reason, sciences, and conscience, and then accepting or rejecting them. The intelligent and knowledgeable ones are those who can read the changing values of their time, and skillfully distill the "right" truths from others.

Stating that our biggest enemy is ignorance, Nursi mentions that it is necessary to study religious and worldly sciences together in order to defeat this enemy and to eliminate bigotry. Nursi states clearly that this is the time of learning and science and encourages people to learn sciences: *"At the end of time, mankind will spill into science and learning. It will obtain all its strength from science. Power and rule will pass to the hand of science."*[15] *"When civilization spreads, science will rule the world."*[16]

---

[12] Ibid., p. 17.
[13] *İşârâtü'l-İ'câz*, p. 105.
[14] Nursi, B. S., *The Letters*, The Twenty-Sixth Letter, p. 376 (translation by Ş. Vahide), accessed September 29, 2014, www.dur.ac.uk/resources/sgia/imeis/Lets24-26.pdf.
[15] Nursi, B. S., *The Words*, The Twentieth Word, p. 272 (translation by Ş. Vahide), accessed September 29, 2014, www.dur.ac.uk/resources/sgia/imeis/words19-22_07_.pdf.
[16] *Âsâr-ı Bediiyye, Nutuklar*, p. 351; *Dîvân-ı Harb-i Örfî*, p. 63.

In addition, he states that the innate duty of man is *"to be perfected through learning"*[17] and his final target is to attain the most comprehensive worship through science, knowledge, and perfection. He also reminds us that man's (Adam's) superiority over angels is through knowledge.

Those who ignore the changing conditions of the world and dream of going back to the past will either adapt to the new conditions or be humiliated. What needs to be done is to evaluate the events and the words in the light of the mind, knowledge, and conscience, before accepting or rejecting them.

Nursi expresses that this is applicable to religious matters, too. He even stated that an exegesis of the Holy Qur'an should be generated by a distinguished committee of selected scholars, each of whom are experts in different fields of science, and not only by scholars of tafsir and Qur'anic exegesis. He also suggested that such a committee should work under the "chairmanship of time," which itself is a great exegete. This is to ensure that events and circumstances are examined in light of the realities of time and necessities of the current conditions. As evidence to his claim, he cites the acceptance of public opinion as valid evidence in Islam:

"Public opinion wants an exegesis of the Qur'an. Yes, every time has a rule (hukm). Time, too, is an exegete. Situations and occurrences are explorers (kashshaf). It is the public opinion of the learnt that can preach the public opinion effectively. On the basis of this subtle point I wish that: Under the chairmanship of time, which itself is a great exegete, an exegesis be written with consultation by an academy of sciences that is formed by the assembly of selected scholars, each of which is a distinguished expert in a separate science. Such an exegesis will combine the beauty and perfection spread out in other exegeses in a purified and gilded manner. Yes, it is constitutionalism; consultation rules in every arena. Public opinion is a safeguard. Validity of the joined opinion of scholars (ijma al-ummah) is a proof to this."[18]

---

[17] Nursi, B. S., *The Words*, The Twenty-Third Word, p. 324 (translation by Ş. Vahide), accessed September 29, 2014, www.dur.ac.uk/resources/sgia/imeis/words23-24_07_.pdf.

[18] *Muhâkemât*, p. 16.

These expressions reflect an innovative point of view that we are not accustomed to. Suggesting that an exegesis of the Qur'an be written for the public by an assembly of highly regarded scholars representing every segment of society is a revolution in the approach to religious matters. Indeed, the statement above and the generalization that consultation rules over everything, including religion, signifies that in this modern era, nothing will stay as it was in the past—even religion, which is the establishment least open to change. If the author of the above words were unknown, one would think that they belonged to a modern and rationalist sociologist with no association with religion. These statements would be disregarded by religious people and the author would be told to mind his own business. However, one has to pay attention to these statements whether one likes them or not, since they belong to a prominent scholar whose contemporaries judged him to be worthy of the title 'Bediüzzaman,' meaning 'the best of the time,' a pious believer who lived his religion with no compromises, and a practitioner who is ahead of all in worship and chastity, and, above all, a worrier who fought with his writings against all attacks that threatened religion.

The emphasis on public opinion, science, and mutual consultation in the above statement, and the attention attracted to these things, leaves no doubt about the importance that should be accorded to modern values in this era of freedom in which we live. Deeming the imaginary personality that represents the required needs and realities of time, which is a 'great exegete' worthy of chairmanship of the committee of scholars assembled to write an exegesis of the Qur'an, is an expression that the familiar scholastic approaches to religion are no longer valid. The weight put on public opinion and consultation with wide participation serves as notice that democracy will serve as a base in decision-making even in religious matters, together with scholars of religion.

Nursi points to wisdom (science), which he defines as a greater good, as the guide that is purified of extremism and shows the moderate way: *"It is an essential maxim affirmed by many that abandoning something in which there is greater good than evil is to commit a greater evil. Since in the past philosophy was polluted with superstition because of ignorance, blind imitation, and the narrow capacity of minds, the scholars of earlier generations urged that philosophy be avoided. However, philosophy embedded in and informed by reported knowledge based on the Divine Revelation, and which also takes into account scientific developments, will surely bring more good than evil. Besides, each time needs a rule."*[19]

That is, even if some harm comes from science, it is little. It is evil and harmful to abandon something in which there is greater good than evil. When it is necessary to choose between two things, the lesser evil is chosen. According to Nursi, people used to keep away from science in the past because science was not developed and there were many wrong things in it; peoples' minds were not at a level to comprehend science and ideas were only imitative; ignorance prevailed. However, science is developed now and has been very useful; thoughts have become free and knowledge prevails. Besides, this age is called the information/knowledge age, and communities are in a process of becoming knowledge-based communities. Therefore, the primary and prevailing judge and guide of this age is science.

Time and the Rule of Time

Man is superficial, and judges on the basis of what he sees on the surface. Therefore, he regards the source of many changes as certain people or events that trigger them. He even attributes extraordinariness to the people or events that seem to be the starters of great movements and sees the changes as their works. Nursi, on the other hand, passes the surface and goes beyond what is visible to the ordinary eye, and draws attention to the invisible engines of change that operate in the background. He turns his attention to the direction and the strength of the blowing wind, and not to the leaves flying around. He looks at the schedule, not the TV screen. He sees the values whose time has come as a time machine that grinds anything on its path.

As those who lack the ability to grasp the values of their time stand against these dominant winds and get blown away, the realists with awakened minds ride these winds and fly to new futures. When projecting the future, Nursi looks at the rising values of the time rather

---

[19] *Muhâkemât*, p. 19.

than the existing balance of power, and passes judgment accordingly. This is because strong currents do the work behind the scenes. Those who resist the currents of time, on the other hand, either stay where they are or get swept away.

One of the values that was dominant in the past but are no longer valid is (using) force. In the past, those who were physically strong and had a strong army used to dominate, and they attained their targets easily. This situation naturally brought about the arms race, and great funds were allocated to defense budgets. However, times have changed. Using force and weapons no longer solves problems; on the contrary, it worsens them, making the solution more difficult. Those who use force lose their strength instead of becoming stronger.

As a matter of fact, the winds of freedom that started to blow strongly at the beginning of the twentieth century became wonderfully effective. Nursi was asked the following question: *"This constitutional monarchy destroyed our administrators but maybe some of them deserved it. They mixed it up with one another by hearing only the name of the constitutional monarchy without seeing anything materially. What is the wisdom behind it?"* He answered as follows:

"Spiritually, there is a rule and ruler of each time. As you put it, there has to be a boss that will make the time machine turn. The ruler of the old times was strength; the one with the sharp sword and a stony heart would rise. But the motor, the soul, the strength, the ruler, and the boss of the times of freedom are righteousness, mind, knowledge, law, and public opinion. Only those with a sharp mind and a bright heart will rise to the top. Since knowledge increases with aging and strength decreases with growing old, the Middle-age states that are based on strength are destined to collapse while the contemporary states being founded on knowledge will have a Khidr-like (eternal) life." "Your bosses, chiefs, and even spiritual leaders, if founded on strength and maintain sharp swords, will necessarily fall, and this is what they deserve. Those who stand on reason, utilize love instead of force, and keep their mind over their emotions, will not fall; they may even rise further."[20]

---

[20] *Münâzarât*, p. 33.

It seems that Nursi saw a century ago the changing values and the course of time that the most clever and learned ones of today cannot see; he expressed it very concisely. He warns those who fail to see the necessities of the time and the direction of the world, and instead, insist on using brutal force rather than the mind, love, and conscience: *"As for the one who strikes with the sword, the sword turns back and hits his own orphans. Now victory is not with the sword. There is a place for the sword, but it is the hand of the mind."*[21] The events in recent years seem to confirm this assessment. Those who resorted to brutal force and even suicide bombers—even for a right cause—are labeled terrorists, and brought misery and tears to their people, rather than victory and happiness. Likewise, even the superpowers who thought they were so powerful that they could do anything but were unaware of the reality of time have hit the invisible wall of time, and shot themselves with their own weapons.

A person who does not know the valid currency of his time and the direction of the course of time rows against the tide; his efforts will go down the drain. In old times, the engine of the time machine was force. But in these modern times, it is the mind, compassion, and conscience, and those who fail to see this will fall down, no matter how strong they are. Their hammer will strike their own heads first. Those who invest in arms and brutal force as they were doing in the past are investing in nothing. Those who invest in the mind, science, research, love, justice, and public opinion will see their investment multiply, and achieve all of their goals easily—even if they are weak in armed forces. Those who think they can achieve their just cause by resorting to brutal force and terror sparked by feelings of revenge and hostility should put aside these negative feelings and reevaluate their approach with a clear mind if they want to put an end to their humiliation and suffering.

It is not the time of emotionalism; it is the time of reason and evidence. In the past, to affect feelings, to narrate one's cause by embellishing and decorating it, was regarded as evidence. However, to resort to something like that today means to go backward. People living today

---

[21] Ibid., p. 68.

take convincing evidence into consideration because it is the rule of this time. As Nursi puts it, *"What generally prevailed in the past and gave rise to spite, enmity, and the complex of being superior were emotions, inclinations, and force. A powerful, convincing speech was enough to guide people. At that time, the ability to embellish a thesis in such a way that it would affect the feelings and inclinations or make it attractive with the power of rhetoric or gestures served for evidence, but comparing ourselves to them means returning to the corners of that time. Every age has a character peculiar to itself. We demand evidence, and are not deceived through the mere statement or embellishment of a thesis."*[22]

---

[22] *Muhâkemât,* p. 25.

Chapter 2

Freedom

The basic feature that makes human beings human, and distinguishes them from the rest of creatures, is the possession of free will, even on a limited scale, and bearing the responsibility of their choices. It can even be said that if it were not for this freedom of choice and the freedom to make wrong choices, humankind would not exist. This is because, from the viewpoint of the philosophy of religion, there already existed plenty of creatures like angels who lack the ability to commit evil, and animals that instinctively perform certain duties like robots without any objection, and creating similar creatures would have been futile. Since God is free of fault, whatever God does, He does it with wisdom and purpose. Humankind owes its existence to the attribute 'freedom,' which is a core value of humanity. Hence, respect to freedom and free will is respect to the existence of humankind. Attempting to abolish freedom and to robotize humankind is an assault on the essence of humanity, and the human nature rejects such an assault. The manner befitting humans is to use their free will in a constructive way, that is, to make the right choices, and in the process to be elevated as human—but to do this using their free will without being subjected to any pressure or compulsion. This is because the age we live in is *"the age of freedom."*[23] Besides, just as it is the *"ugliness of the ugly that increases the beauty of the beautiful,"*[24] so is the lowliness of the low—those who

---

[23] Nursi, B. S., *The Letters*, The Twenty-Ninth Letter, p. 493 (translation by Ş. Vahide), accessed September 29, 2014, www.dur.ac.uk/resources/sgia/imeis/Lets29_2_SofR.pdf.

[24] *Mesnevî-i Nuriye*, p. 196.

make their choices in accordance with their wants and desires—that increase the highness of the high. The continuation of the human race depends on the simultaneous existence of these two lines of preferences.

When it comes to advocating freedom, Nursi does not fall behind the Western proponents of freedom. His expression "*I can live without bread, but not without freedom*"[25] leaves no doubt about his addiction to freedom. At the same time, he emphasizes the necessity for drawing the limits of freedom, which is the reason for our existence, correctly so as to benefit both individuals and humanity the most. According to Nursi, "*If the cure is taken to excess, it becomes the cause of ill, and is fatal.*"[26] There is a similar saying in the West: 'The difference between medicine and poison is its dosage.' Nursi sees absolute freedom as savagery and animalism: "*Absolute freedom, however, is absolute savagery; indeed, it is animalism. From the point of view of humanity, too, freedom has to be restricted.*"[27]

He defines freedom as "*being free in its broadest sense*" within the law and fairness, and restraining from any oppression and compulsion: "*Perhaps freedom is this: apart from the law of justice and reprimand, no one should dominate over others. The rights of every individual should be protected, and everyone should be eminently free in their legitimate acts.*"[28] Although everything is free, he reminds people that they are still slaves of Allah: "*People have become free but they are still slaves of Allah. Everything has become free; Sharia is free and so is constitutional monarchy.*"[29]

The entire modern world is unanimous on the need to restrict freedom; however, opinions vary on the manner and the amount of the restrictions. The common approach in the West is that one's freedom ends where others' start. That is, no one has the right or freedom to harm others or violate their freedom. Therefore, violating others' rights is a universal crime. Nursi redefines the borders of freedom so as to include

---

[25] *Tarihçe-i Hayat*, p. 458.
[26] *Sözler*, Lemeât, p. 783.
[27] *Hutbe-i Şâmiye*, p. 96.
[28] *Münâzarât*, p. 20.
[29] *Hutbe-i Şâmiye*, p. 88.

the individual: "*The essence of freedom is that: one should harm neither himself nor others.*"[30] This is because, when viewed from the perspective of belief in God, the human body belongs to God, who is its Maker, and it is given to the person as a trust of God. Harming this entrusted being and using it outside the area permitted by its Owner is a breach of trust, and an abuse of freedom. Even the Western world has limited, although just partially, one's freedom to harm oneself by some laws and law enforcement measures such as banning or seriously limiting the use of narcotic drugs, alcohol, and cigarettes. However, such external bans are far from being effective.

The approach that is commensurate with the age of freedom is for any ban to come from within the individual by preference rather than from outside by compulsion. This can be achieved most effectively with a strong and conscious belief: "*Belief places in the heart and mind a permanent 'prohibitor.' When sinful desires emerge from the soul, it repulses them, declaring: 'it is forbidden!'*"[31]

Nursi rejects the understanding of freedom expressed as "*nothing would be told to those committing debauchery and ignominy as long as they do not harm others,*" and he labels this understanding not as freedom, but to the contrary, as captivity: "*Freedom of debauchery and ignominy is not freedom. It might be animalism, or oppression of the Devil, or captivity to the evil-commanding soul.*"[32] Those whose primary aim in life is to satisfy their desires are not much different from the animals doing the same thing. Indeed, those sharing this view of life define humans as intelligent, social, or economic animals. Besides, the bad habits and addictions that have become one of the global problems of our time and exceed the will power of people—such as alcoholism, gambling, smoking, narcotic drugs, entertainment, and even chocolate and compulsive shopping—have strangled people like an octopus and captivated them. People realize this captivity when they attempt to break loose from these bad habits. Nursi points out the irony of those who think they are enjoying their freedom to the fullest by going after their desires

---

[30] *Münâzarât*, p. 19.
[31] *Hutbe-i Şâmiye*, p. 76.
[32] *Münâzarât*, p. 19.

and fancy: *"Sometimes opposites conceal their opposites.... Enslavement to the animal passions and the despotism of Satan have been called freedom."*[33]

Nursi defines freedom in the Islamic scope as bridling the soul and urging the spirit to sublime matters; he states that it will bring about real humanity and happiness in the world and the hereafter: *"As for The wisdom of the Qur'an, its aims are to place a barrier before the illicit assaults of the soul's base appetites and to urge the spirit to sublime matters, to satisfy man's elevated emotions and encourage him towards the human perfections ... And the result of reining in and tethering the evil-commanding soul and leaving the spirit free and urging it towards perfection is happiness in this world and the next."*[34] *"However, the freedom which is as bright as the sun, loved by all spirits, the equivalent of the essence of humanity is the freedom which has lived in the felicific palace of the civilization and has been embellished with knowledge, virtues, Islamic education and garments."*[35] He describes the freedom except the one described above as oppression, slavery, or savagery. *"The freedom outside the scope of the Sharia is oppression or slavery to one's soul or brutal animalism or savagery."*[36]

Nursi forces the limits in the understanding of freedom and mentions the freedom of non-living things like the sun: *"The Divine Power has made everything movable and condemned nothing to immobility or inertia. Thus, the Divine Mercy did not bind the sun up in inertia, which is the brother of death and the cousin of non-existence. Therefore, the sun is free, and can freely travel in obedience to the Divine law, on condition that it does not violate the freedom of others. The sun is a general of the desert that is formed by Divine Command and that applies all of its acts based on Divine Will."*[37] To express it more simply, there is life in movement; to remain fixed in one's place and being a status quo supporter

---

[33] *Sözler*, Lemeât, p. 770.

[34] Nursi, B. S., *The Words*, The Twenty-Fifth Word, p. 421 (translation by Ş. Vahide), accessed September 29, 2014, www.dur.ac.uk/resources/sgia/imeis/words25_07_.pdf.

[35] *Münâzarât*, p. 21.

[36] *Hutbe-i Şâmiye*, p. 96.

[37] *Muhâkemât*, pp. 58–59.

is death and non-existence. The sun is free as long as it acts in its orbit in accordance with laws of physics and it does not move to the orbits of other stars; it is virtually the king of the area it moves in.

Nursi points to the fact that the animals that live in the mountains have freedom mixed with savagery: "*In fact, if these animals have some pleasure and consolation, it originates from their freedom.*"[38] The existence of freedom is pleasure for man; lack of freedom is torture for him. Therefore, to limit freedom, that is, to send people to prison, is a common punishment in the modern world.

On the other hand, Nursi mentions academic freedom in the most modern sense; he regards it as a necessity of democracy that scientific research, publications and views be free from all kinds of influences and pressures. "*This academic freedom cannot be restricted by any means in the period of Republic.*"[39] Nursi acclaims the independent scientific research made based on objectivity by leaving prejudice aside: "*Well done to the efforts of the exact sciences; they tore down the despotic Greek philosophy.*"[40]

Nursi sees freedom as a property of belief and states that the compassion and solemnity originating from belief prevents a person from suppressing others or being suppressed by others. "*For a man who becomes a servant of the Master of Universe by embracing faith, his self-respect and heroism of faith will never let him lower himself before others, and accept to serve under the rule of an oppressor. Likewise, the compassion that stems from his faith will not allow him to violate the rights and freedoms of others. Yes, a righteous servant of a Sultan will not lower himself as to accept the dominance of a shepherd. That servant will also hold himself above dominating a helpless person. So the more perfect the faith is, the brighter the sun of freedom shines. Here is the time of the Age of Happiness.*"[41]

Nursi draws attention to the bigotry and anti-freedom sentiment coming from religion, and as an example, he points to those who attacked

---

[38] *Münâzarât*, p. 21.
[39] *Tarihçe-i Hayat*, p. 215.
[40] *Muhâkemât*, p. 60.
[41] *Münâzarât*, p. 23.

Sultan Abdulhamid, famous for his oppressive rule, with a totally contrary claim that *"he is wicked for accepting freedom and constitution thirty years ago."*[42] Among these, there were even some who crossed the line to the extreme and accused the law makers with infidelity for not using the Qur'an as the source, citing the Qur'anic verse, "If any do fail to judge by (the light of) what God hath revealed, they are (no better than) Unbelievers . . ." as proof. Nursi described these foes as the wretched who do not know that the phrase "those who do fail to judge" means "those who do not affirm," and expressed his reaction as follows: *"How can I not object to those who confuse the past oppression with freedom and object the constitution?" In appearance, they opposed the government, but what they asked for was a more severe oppression. That is why I rejected them. The ones that allege the freedom supporters to have gone astray are from among those."*[43] Bigotry expressed in the name of religion set the stage for the supporters of Westernization to attack religion: "They did not know religion; they were unjustly opposing the followers of Islam, and were citing oppression as justification."[44] This environment of quarrel has harmed the country for a century, and it still does.

Nursi objects to those who claim, "The Islamic Unity, which aims the Sunnah of Prophet Muhammad, peace and blessings be upon him, limits freedom and it is contrary to the necessities of the civilization." He tells them that a person who is the slave of God Almighty will not be a slave of others: *"Belief necessitates not humiliating others through oppression and despotism and not degrading them, and, secondly, not belittling oneself before tyrants."*[45] *"In fact, the believer is completely free. A person who is the slave of the Creator of this realm does not abase himself people. The stronger belief gets, the stronger freedom gets."*[46] That is, belief and freedom are directly proportional not inversely.

Answering the question of why Islamic truths did not remain sovereign fully in the past and what would change in the future, Nursi says

[42] Ibid., p. 22.
[43] Ibid., p. 83.
[44] Ibid., p. 83.
[45] *Hutbe-i Şâmiye*, p. 60.
[46] Ibid., p. 96.

people will eliminate the domination forced on behalf of the religion and will question everything by abandoning imitation as a result of the increase of the idea of freedom and the tendency to search the truths: *"The domination and arbitrary power of the clergy and religious leaders, and the fact that the Europeans obeyed and followed them blindly. These two obstacles have also started to disappear with the rise among mankind of the idea of freedom, and the desire to search for the truth."*[47]

The correct level of freedom is directly proportional to the level of development, especially the level of development in reasoning. To give freedom to children who cannot yet distinguish between right and wrong, benefit and harm, the wolf and the lamb, does not mean to free them; it means to make them vulnerable to the wolves. Therefore, the restriction of the freedom of a child by parents at home and by the state in the community (like compulsory school attendance, prohibition of buying alcoholic drinks and cigarettes before a certain age) are not oppression but compassion; and it is a world standard. As children, who are completely dependent on their parents when they are born, grow up, their freedom grows, too. When they are about eighteen, both of them become mature enough. To impose restrictions on the freedom of the people who have reached a certain age and who have obtained enough knowledge and skill for correct reasoning with the pretext of "protection" will be more harmful than useful; and will demotivate them, prevent their abilities from developing and will suppress them.

Humanity is also developing just like a person and it also has phases like childhood and adulthood. *"There is rising to perfection in humanity."*[48] *"In the tree of the world is the desire to be perfected. That is, all atoms and organs of man are inclined to perfection and proceed toward perfection."*[49] It is possible to understand the restriction of freedom, the prevalence of prohibitions and the strictness of rules during the period of childhood aiming to prevent children from being deceived and doing harmful things. However, humanity ended the period of childhood and has entered the period of adulthood now. His mind and reasoning have

---

[47]   Ibid., p. 28.
[48]   *İşârâtü'l-İ'câz*, p. 49.
[49]   Ibid., p. 119.

developed; education and science have formed a healthy common ground. In a time when winds of freedom blow globally, it is reactionary and backward to resort to prohibitions by fearing freedom. Yes, in the environment of freedom, there will be some people who will be harmed by using their preferences in a wrong way. However, these harms will not be very significant compared to the benefits brought about by freedom. It is very harmful to abandon something that will be very useful, fearing a small harm: *"The lesser evil is acceptable for the greater good. If an evil which will lead to a greater good is abandoned so that a lesser evil should not be, a greater evil will then have been perpetrated."*[50] With this concise expression, Nursi teaches us to approach events holistically and to judge, taking the whole into consideration.

He holds the view that freedom will become widespread in the world and it will eliminate suppression and despotism: *"When the freedom scale of the balance ascend, savagery and despotism will descend; it will gradually disappear."*[51] He gives the following answer to the hypochondriacs who live with the fear that other countries are looking for opportunities to tear our country into pieces and swallow it by ignoring the fact that colonialism ended as freedom developed: *"Do not be afraid! As civilization, virtue, and freedom become more and more dominant in the world of humanity, the other side of the balance will necessarily get lighter and lighter."*[52] However, the general level of democracy in a community or country is a result of the democracy level of its individuals. For, *"General freedom is the product of the freedom particles of individuals."*[53] Therefore, the level of freedom in a country is closely related to the level of the perception of freedom in the minds rather than laws.

Nursi gives the following exemplary answer to those who panic due to the freedoms given to non-Muslim minorities like the Armenians and Greeks in the process that began with the Reform Era in the Otto-

---

[50] Nursi, B. S., *The Letters*, The Twelfth Letter, p. 59 (translation by Ş. Vahide), accessed September 29, 2014, www.dur.ac.uk/resources/sgia/imeis/Lets1-13.pdf.
[51] *Münâzarât*, p. 27.
[52] Ibid., p. 29.
[53] Ibid., p. 19.

man State: *"Their freedom is not to oppress them and to leave them alone. It is in compliance with Islam . . . Suppose that their freedom is bad for you. However, it is not harmful for Muslims. For, the number of the Armenians living in our country is no more than three million and all of the number of the non-Muslims is not more than ten million. However, the number of Muslims is more than three hundred million; they get tied with three terrible bonds of despotism and are crushed under the slavery of the spiritual pressure of the foreigners. The freedom of non-Muslims, which is one part of our freedom, is the bribe for the freedom of our whole nation. And it is the expeller of the spiritual despotism. And it is the key to those cuffs. And it is the remover of the terrible spiritual despotism imposed on us by the foreigners."*[54] Nursi teaches us here that it is necessary to look at events holistically, not in isolation, and that it is necessary to give priority to reasoning; he focuses on possible results.

Nursi draws attention to the necessity of giving freedom in the broadest sense in the republican regime and he complains about the so-called freedom under the name of republic: *"If I stayed in prison, the most comfortable place of a brutal government, whose freedom is only ostensible freedom."*[55] He wanted freedoms to be given without any discrimination, in accordance with the spirit of the republican regime: *"In the republican government that gives the widest form of freedom, I am denied all kinds of freedom but my enemies act against me and crush me freely. The republican government that ensures freedom of thought and conscience and scientific freedom should protect me fully and silence my hypochondriac enemies or should give me freedom of writing and expression like my enemies without preventing my defense."*[56] Nursi was always an advocate of all kinds of freedom primarily the freedom of conscience and thought; he regarded the republican regime applied correctly as the guarantee for freedom.

---

[54] Ibid., p. 25.
[55] *Tarihçe-i Hayat*, p. 59.
[56] *Emirdağ Lahikası-1*, p. 23.

Chapter 3

Democracy and Republic

The presence of deeply rooted prejudices and misunderstandings even in this age of information is truly unfortunate for humanity. Many people, for instance, religious or not, still believe that religiosity and being democratic are opposites of one another, and cannot coexist. Similarly, many believe that a democratic government cannot be compatible with Islam; and because of this blood mismatch, Islam poses a potential threat to democratic regimes. A good number of people believe that religious people who seem to be democratic are really not sincere, and the first thing they will do if given a chance is to demolish democracy and reestablish the sultanate. Because of this baseless presumption, sincere pious people have been perceived as a threat called reactionary (backwardness) for a century now, and any rise in religiosity or strengthening of pious people have fueled such baseless fears. These people with profound suspicions think that even Nursi is hostile to democracy for dedicating his entire life to religion and serving religion, and include millions of Nursi's students in this baseless presumption for reading his works. Nursi's life and works, on the other hand, refute such suppositions and show the opposite to be true.

Even during sultanate, Nursi declared that sultanate was an institution that has completed its time, and he applauded the declaration of constitutionalism that ended oppression, and encouraged everyone to support it. He did this not in spite of religion, but rather, in the name of religion. For instance, when Nursi was asked by the Kurdish tribes in the East in 1911, *"Will there not be any more sultans who reigned like Sultan Hamid? Will there not be the old way any longer?"* he answered with the question, *"If this black tent of yours were torn into little pieces and burned, and its ashes were scattered in the air, is it at all possible to make a new tent from those ashes, and reside in it?"*[57], indicating elegantly that the sultanate or monarchy is gone forever, never to return. He cites public awakening as the reason for this change: *"Despite the fact that there were only ten heedful people among a thousand, oppression with all its mighty power could not stand against it, and crumbled. Now the strength of oppression has declined to one from a thousand; vigilance and awakening of minds have risen from one to a thousand."*[58]

When Nursi was asked in Afyon Court, *"What do you think of the Republic?"* he replied: *"As my biography which you have in your hands proves, I was a religious republican before any of you, with the exception of the Chairman of the Court, was born. A summary is this: like now, I was living at that time in seclusion in a remote tomb. They used to bring me soup, and I would give breadcrumbs to the ants. I used to eat my bread having dipped it in the soup. They asked me about it and I told them: the ant and bee nations are republicans. I give the breadcrumbs to the ants out of respect for their republicanism. Then they said to me: 'You are opposing the righteous early generations of Islam.' I told them in reply: 'The four Rightly-Guided Caliphs were both Caliphs and Presidents of the Republic. Abu Bakr the Veracious, may God be pleased with him, the Ten Promised Paradise, and the Companions of the Prophet were like presidents of the republic. But not as an empty name and title, they were heads of a religious republic which bore the meaning of true justice and freedom in accordance with the Sharia.'"*[59]

These expressions alone show clearly that Nursi was a republican long before the establishment of the Turkish Republic, that he reconciled democracy with religion from his early years, as indicated by the phrase "a religious republican," and that he saw republicanism as the regime most compatible with Islam. He states that the Rightly Guided Four Caliphs, who were elected by the members of the first Islamic

---

[57] *Münâzarât*, p. 52.

[58] Ibid., p. 52.

[59] Nursi, B. S., *The Rays*, The Fourteenth Ray, pp. 385–386 (translation by Ş. Vahide), accessed September 29, 2014, www.dur.ac.uk/resources/sgia/imeis/14Ray07.pdf.

community with their free will, were presidents in the real sense, and he cites this application in the purest and earliest era of Islam as a proof that the regime most suitable to the essence of Islam is republicanism, not monarchy. The early Muslims' determination of their presidents by election while monarchism was the rule all over the world, and being able to use their preference for someone who is not coming from the kin of the Prophet is highly significant as it shows that the Companions of the Prophet, known for being the most pious of all, were also the most democratic people.

The fact that the governing systems were changed to monarchies later on is not due to Islam, but rather, due to the unfavorable conditions of those times, and such regimes have found widespread acceptance in the name of continuity and stability—until the winds of freedom started to blow and favorable conditions for a democratic government are reestablished. Pointing to the antidemocratic regimes that are widespread in the Middle East and are contrary to the essence of Islam as 'Islamic regimes' is absolute ignorance if not ill-intention.

The essence of real democracy is freedom in its broadest sense, starting with the freedom of expression and practicing free consultation in decision making, rather than yielding to the imposition of a person or a group. Indeed, republicanism is a regime of consultation with the public. Nursi points to the Qur'an as the source of republicanism and quotes the following verses as proof to his claim: "*they conduct their affairs by mutual consultation,*" (ash-Shura 42:38) and "*consult with them in your affairs*" (Al Imran 3:159).[60] The Prophet has interpreted these verses in the best way possible with his actions during his lifetime by making it a rule in governing to consult with the prominent members of the community, and following the majority opinion even when it is against his own (as it happened with the decision regarding the Battle of Uhud). A feature of modern democracies is to reach decisions at all levels by the meeting of the individuals involved or their representatives, and to hold meetings in an environment of absolute freedom of expression with the assurance that even the most opposing views

---

[60] *Sünûhât*, p. 31.

can freely be stated. Otherwise, the so-called consultation meetings where leaders announce their own views with the expectation of approval by the membership, or meetings during which the attendees take position by the expressed opinion of the leader, are pure formalism, and not democracy. It is monarchy painted with democracy.

Nursi mentions the importance of consultation and the Qur'an's ordering consultation as a fundamental principle in many places; he even regards history lessons as consultation with previous generations: *"The key to Muslims' happiness in Islamic social life is the mutual consultation enjoined by the Sharia. The verse, 'Whose rule is consultation among themselves (ash-Shura 42:38)' orders consultation as a fundamental principle. Just as the consultation of the ages and centuries that mankind has practiced by means of history, a conjunction of ideas, formed the basis of the progress and sciences of all mankind, so too one reason for the backwardness of Asia, the largest continent, was the failure to practice that true consultation."*[61]

Nursi explains his keenness on constitutionalism based on justice and consultation (republicanism) as follows: *"My addiction to and love for the meaning constitutionalism is that the first door of development of Asia and the Islamic world in the future is freedom within the framework of religious principles. The key to the fate, sovereignty and bliss of Islam is also consultation in constitutionalism."*[62] *"The key and discloser of the continent of Asia and its future is mutual consultation."*[63]

Nursi pointed out the changing times back in early 1900s, and stated that the time for one-man rule—sultanate and caliphate—has passed, and that it was time for public-rule based on consultation rather than individual dictatorship for both state and religious affairs: *"We no longer live in old times. In the past the ruler was a single person. That ruler's mufti could likewise be a single person who corrected or changed the ruler's judgment. But now is the time for community. The ruler is a collective spirit that emerges from the community's spirit, which is some-*

---

[61] *Hutbe-i Şâmiye,* p. 60.
[62] *Tarihçe-i Hayat,* pp. 74–75.
[63] *Hutbe-i Şâmiye,* p. 60.

what deaf, has little sensitivity, but has strong collective personality, and councils represent that spirit."[64]

In his last sentence, Nursi describes the essence of republicanism, and expresses elegantly that it is the public opinion that rules in a real democracy. He also explains that the main function of councils, which are assemblies that consist of representatives, is to represent public opinion. That is, a parliament should be such a body that public opinion is its spirit, public will is the driver, and it is the public that rules in the personality of the parliament. And this should be so not only for state affairs, but religious affairs as well. This philosophy should be the guiding principle for all institutions, small or large. In such a system that is truly democratic, the identity and the ideology of the president does not matter much since the main role of a president is to apply the decisions made by the group as if they are his own decisions. That is, to serve as an "executive officer." Therefore, in real democracies, there is no imposition or compulsion coming from above (which are often rejected since they cause reactions, low morale, and reduced productivity); rather, there are directives rising from below.

Pointing out that consultation rules over everything, Nursi expresses that an exegesis of the Holy Qur'an should be written by a consultation committee of scholars representing every segment of the society: "*It is necessary to establish a committee consisting of investigative scientists and experts with broad minds and fine views for the discovery of the meanings of the Qur'an, bringing together its separate beauties and determination of the Qur'anic truths that appear with the passing of time and inventions by science.*

"*To sum up: It is necessary for the person to interpret the Qur'an to have a high genius, a penetrating and profound power of making judgments and a holy power. In this age, such a person can only be a spiritual personality, which can emerge from the union and solidarity of many spirits, the union of ideas, mutual assistance, and the reflection of hearts and sincerity of the members of the committee mentioned above. It will be the spiritual soul of that committee.*

---

[64] *Sünûhât*, p. 33.

"Yes, as the saying goes, 'there is a property that exists in the collection of something but it does not exist in all of the individuals that form the collection.' The works of ijtihad and the properties and light of the luminous light of sainthood is seen in a congregation but they are not seen in any of the individual. It means the sincere solidarity of ordinary men produces the property of sainthood."[65]

When there is real democracy, the question, "Who is the head of the family?" is meaningless because the leader of a democratic family is not a person but a spiritual collective personality that consists of the common spirit of the family. Everybody, including the apparent head of the family, is an organ of this common spirit and they fulfill their duties and responsibilities. In a democratic family, all of the decisions are made by consultation through the participation of the members of the whole family including older children; and when necessary, the views of experts outside the family are also considered. What the shrewd person selected as the head of the family needs to do is to apply the decisions democratically and not to dominate the other members.

Nursi states that all forms of leadership, including presidency, are indeed servanthood, and he bases this notion on a hadith that he views as a constitution of Islam: *"In fact, a hadith which is a constitution of Islam states, 'The chief of a nation is the one who serves its citizens'; that is, public officials and administrators are not chiefs, but servants to people. Democracy and freedom of conscience can be based on this fundamental law of Islam."*[66] While many Muslim thinkers have had a difficult time trying to reconcile Islam and democracy, Nursi based freedom of conscience, which forms the foundation of secular governments along with democracy, on this fundamental law of Islam, and presented democracy and freedom of conscience among basic human rights and freedoms. That is, in the true democracies, in which the administrators of the state are servants not despots, mentioned in the hadith, people determine what to believe in using their own free wills and consciences; and the state assures the individuals to have the freedom of choosing and practicing their beliefs.

---

[65] *Emirdağ Lahikası-2*, p. 83.
[66] *Emirdağ Lahikası-2*, p. 150.

Nursi introduces consultation as one of the three legs of a republic, and emphasizes the necessity that justice be taken as foundation, and power be confined in the law. Otherwise, arbitrary ruling and tyranny would prevail: *"Republicanism consists of justice, mutual consultation, and the confinement of power in the law. Power must reside within the law. Otherwise, despotism will spread out."*[67]

He mentions justice, honesty, and equality before law as the requisites of constitutionalism, which he used in the sense of republicanism before: *"The so called constitutionalism will last forever on the principles of justice, honesty, and abolishing of privileges."*[68] He explains the reasons for the abolishment of privileges as follows: *"So that, one does not sow discord with a privilege he has, by looking down on others as pests."*[69]

Nursi claims that the fundamental principles of constitutionalism (republicanism) could be deduced from Islam: *"I claimed that it is possible to deduce the truths of constitutionalism explicitly, implicitly, permissibly, from the Four Schools of Islamic Law."*[70] This way, he establishes clearly that there could be no conflict or dissonance between Islam and constitutionalism (in the sense of republicanism). In fact, he equates constitutionalism with sharia in some way, stating that both are opposites of despotism and oppression: *"Despotism is tyranny and oppression. Constitutionalism is justice and sharia."*[71] *"The real path of true sharia is the truth of constitutionalism that conforms to sharia."*[72] In simpler words, it is possible to look at sharia as republicanism, and republicanism as sharia when justice is taken as the basis. While many Muslim scholars opposed constitutionalism on the grounds that it is incompatible with sharia, Nursi took the opposite stand: *"I accepted constitutionalism with proof from sharia."*[73]

---

[67]   *Hutbe-i Şâmiye*, p. 88.
[68]   *Tarihçe-i Hayat*, p. 70.
[69]   Ibid., p. 69.
[70]   Ibid., p. 62.
[71]   Ibid., p. 61.
[72]   Ibid., p. 60.
[73]   Ibid.

In the third year of constitutional rule, Nursi answered the question, *"What is constitutionalism?"* as *"sovereignty of people,"* again signifying that he uses the term constitutionalism in the sense of republicanism, and defines it as follows: *"Constitutionalism is sovereignty of people. That is, the elected representatives that are the embodied form of public opinion rule, and the government is a service provider and thus a servant."*[74] *"Constitutionalism is sovereignty of people; you also have become rulers. It is bliss for all nations; you too will attain happiness. It awakens all enthusiasm and exalted emotions."*[75] He continues: *"The essence of constitutionalism is that power lies within the law, and the individual is nothing. The basis of despotism is that power lies with an individual, who can subject the law to his will—the defeat of justice by power."*[76]

Nursi tells his contemporaries that they have slept enough and warns that it is time to wake up. He states that republicanism turns humanity to true humanity by elevating it from animalism, and that it is the key to progress: *"This much sleep is enough; you too need to wake up. Republicanism saves a human from animalism; you too become fully human. It will unlock Islam's good fortune and Asia's fate."*[77]

Nursi cites the Qur'an as the source of constitutionalism in the sense of republicanism, and describes it as a system of mutual consultation, justice, sciences, love, and 'law-based instead of individual-based': *"Here, constitutionalism is the manifestation of the Qur'anic verses 'And consult them in affairs of public concern' (Al Imran 3:159) and 'They conduct their affairs in consultation among themselves' (ash-Shura 42:38) and consultation enjoined by the sharia. This luminous body's life is truth in place of force; its heart is knowledge, its tongue is love; its mind is the law, not an individual."*[78]

Nursi was a lover of freedom and republicanism though he was tried several times based on the claims that he was not (he was acquitted on all charges); in 1911, he praised republicanism under the name

---

[74] *Münâzarât*, p. 42.
[75] Ibid., p. 23.
[76] Ibid., p. 38.
[77] Ibid., p. 23.
[78] Ibid., p. 23.

of constitutional monarchy a lot and regarded republicanism, which elevated everybody virtually to the level of a sultan, as the most important requirement of humanity: *"The despotic administration based on the view of one person, which can be turned to any direction like a thin wire is transformed into the view of the people which is like an unshakable iron mast and an always sharp diamond sword; trust it like Noah's Ark. It makes everybody like a sultan; try to be a sultan by advocating freedom. It ensures and frees man's free will, which is the essence of humanity; do not consent to being stagnant."*[79]

Nursi sees the democratic atmosphere provided by constitutionalism (republicanism) as a platform of progress, enlightenment and creativity: *"Before the real sunrise of the constitutionalism, I was illiterate and inexperienced in terms of writing books."*[80] Nursi also says, *"In the past, there was only one view; nobody asked the nation what they wanted; now, it is the era of consultation; the view of people is asked."*[81] He gives the following comprehensive answer to those who regard constitutionalism as a simple right of speech and who criticize him stating that he has gone to extremes: *"When constitutional administration is in effect, freedom of thought awakens constitutionalism in all aspects. It brings about a kind of constitutionalism in all species and groups related to its art. It even results in a kind of constitutionalism in scholars, religious schools and students. Yes, every group is inspired a constitutionalism and a regeneration peculiar to them. What make me love the government of constitution are the gleams of consultation that show the sun of happiness and that start to incline, be attracted and be integrated."*[82]

Nursi sees the source of the wrong sects in the religion as despotism in science and states that these sects will move to the right path when constitutionalism in science (in other words, academic freedom) is established fully. *"In my opinion, what produced the groups like Mutazila, Jabriyya, Murjia and Mujassima that deviated from Islam by starting imitation and causing clash of ideas is the academic despotism in*

---

[79] Ibid., p. 24.
[80] Ibid., p. 16.
[81] Ibid., p. 31.
[82] Ibid., p. 31

religious issues and in fact freedom in the restricted things. If academic freedom is established truly, it is strongly hoped that the wrong and deviant sects and groups will join Ahl as-Sunnah and Jama'ah with the help of the tendency to search the truth, true sciences and fairness. Those sects do not seem like parties but they have spread through their ideas. Everybody may have an inclination to their way. If a brain were enlarged and if meanings were embodied, that separation would be seen in that brain like a cinema film."[83] That is, according to Nursi, freedom and republicanism will free the minds from the influence of wrong movements and groups.

Nursi stresses that Islam has no connection with bigotry that originates from ignorance and lack of reasoning, and adds that those who claim otherwise are in deeper bigotry: "*What is becoming of Islam is strength of piety, which is fortitude, perseverance, and adhering to righteousness. It is not at all bigotry that stems from a lack of reasoning. To me, the most horrifying type of bigotry is that found in some European enthusiasts and irreligious people who stubbornly dwell on their superficial doubts. It is unlike the way of the scholars of Islam, who embrace with evidence and proof.*"[84]

Nursi responded to the question "*What is despotism?*" with this remarkable answer defining despotism along with its characteristics: "*Despotism is oppression. It is dealing with others in an arbitrary fashion. It is compulsion relying on force. It is the opinion of one person. It provides extremely favorable ground for exploitation. It is the basis of tyranny. It annihilates humanity. It is despotism which reduces man to the most abject valleys of abasement; it has caused the Islamic world to sink into abjection and degradation, which arouses animosity and malice, has poisoned Islam . . .*"[85] He even went further, naming oppression "*fatal poison.*"[86] Associating Islam with despotism is the overturning of the truth.

---

[83] Ibid., p. 32.

[84] Ibid., p. 89.

[85] Ibid., p. 22.

[86] Ibid.

Nursi opposed all forms of despotism regardless of where it comes from and whatever its name is. He supported every step taken towards freedom and democracy such as the constitutionalism that is based on mutual consultation and people's participation in governance and the declaration of the first constitution protecting individual rights and freedoms. He also asked people to be supportive of these efforts: *"Constitutionalism and the constitution about which you have heard consist of true justice and the consultation enjoined by the sharia. Consider it favorably and work to preserve it; for, our worldly happiness lies in constitutionalism. And we have suffered more than anyone from despotism."*[87]

In a speech addressed to deputies in Hagia Sophia, Nursi advised them: *"Regard and present constitutionalism in the name of legitimacy (which is in accordance with sharia.)"*[88] During the final years of the Ottomans, while many prominent people of that period opposed constitutionalism in the name of religion and showed their reactions on March 31, 1909, rebellion, Nursi applauded constitutionalism and the constitution in the name of Islam, and was extremely disturbed that Islam was being associated with despotism.

Nursi explained and corrected the article he had written in 1909 addressing members of parliament later (1954) stating that what he meant by constitutionalism was republicanism and democracy: *"Constitutionalism in the sense of republicanism and democracy, justice and consultation called constitution and gathering the power in laws . . ."*[89] Here, he explains the understanding of constitution as providing justice, compromising by negotiation and making laws and rules that represent social compromise dominant by leaving persons out. This understanding is in full compliance with the understanding of constitution in modern democratic communities.

Nursi expresses that the source of advocacy for despotism is ignorance and bigotry, not Islam: *"Tyranny is not the fault of constitutionalism; it may well be the result of the darkness of ignorance in your head. . . . Yes, if the citizens of a nation do not know their rights due to their*

---

[87] *Tarihçe-i Hayat*, p. 60.
[88] Ibid., p. 62.
[89] *Dîvân-ı Harb-i Örfî*, p. 69.

ignorance, they would lead even patriotic people to despotism."[90] *"I was extremely saddened deep in my heart that Europe, with the allowance of the ignorance and bigotry within us, held the notion that sharia (God forbid!) was suitable for despotism. In order to refute their supposition, I applauded constitutionalism on behalf of sharia more than anyone else."*[91] In various speeches to scholars and students, Nursi explained that, *"tyrannous despotism has no connection with sharia,"* and expressed the implication of a hadith as *"the sharia came to the world in order to extirpate oppression and despotic tyranny."*[92]

Nursi tells those who object to the equality with non-Muslims ensured by the constitution that everybody is equal before law and gives some examples of the sultans and the kings in the past being tried with ordinary non-Muslims: *"Equality is not in honor and virtue—it is before law. A king and a slave are equal before law. Curiously, if a Divine law cautions against knowingly stepping on ants, restrains from tormenting them, how can it neglect the rights of human beings? Never ... We did not conform to this rule. Yes, the trial of Ali, may God be pleased with him, with an ordinary Jew, and our pride Salahaddin Ayyubi's court challenge with an ordinary Christian should correct your misunderstanding, I believe."*[93]

Nursi points out that in this age opposites often take the place of one another: *"There are some changes in some truths today. Opposites have taken the place of one another. Oppression is called justice; jihad is called rebellion and slavery is called freedom."*[94] However, he draws attention to the fact that *"Truths will not change by changing their names."*[95] Therefore, he focused his attention on the features of constitutionalism and republicanism rather than their names, and rejected any form of despotism and oppression dressed in constitutionalism or republicanism: *"Since I have taken an oath on the attributes of legitimate and*

---

[90] *Münâzarât*, p. 28.
[91] *Tarihçe-i Hayat*, p. 61.
[92] Ibid., p. 60.
[93] *Münâzarât*, p. 30.
[94] *Sünûhât*, p. 81.
[95] *Tarihçe-i Hayat*, p. 70.

true constitutionalism, I will slap despotism when I encounter it no matter what form it comes in—even if it is presented and named constitutionalism."[96] Nursi took a stand against pseudo-constitutionalism which *"consists of the despotism of a party"* and is *"named constitutionalism but means despotism,"*[97] and declared that the real enemies of constitutionalism are those who antagonize the public against it by misusing it: *"In my opinion, the enemies of constitutionalism are those who increase its enemies by portraying constitutionalism as cruel, hideous, and contrary to sharia."*[98] In 1911, Nursi answers a question related to the source of the good deeds and bad deeds as follows: *"All of the present good deeds come from the light of constitutionalism and all of the bad deeds come from that darkness of the previous despotism or the oppression of a new despotism called constitutionalism. What is left for it is to follow its father by bidding farewell after expressing condolence."*[99]

The practices of despotism carried out under the name of constitutionalism during the power of the Party of Union and Progress continues during the period of republic, too. As a matter of fact, Nursi expresses the problems caused by the practices contrary to the essence of the republic as follows in a petition he writes to Afyon court: *"Calling absolute despotism 'the Republic' in order to attack us, and making the regime a screen to absolute apostasy, and calling absolute dissipation 'civilization,' and calling arbitrary compulsion on account of disbelief 'the law,' our enemies have both ruined us, and deceived the government, and preoccupied the judiciary with us for no reason."*[100]

Lastly, Nursi mentions the conditions necessary for the settlement of constitutionalism in the sense of republicanism and everybody's making use of it to the utmost as purification from savagery, ignorance, and enmity. As a matter of fact, he answers the question asked by the tribes in 1911, *"How much of the constitutionalism you are describing has come*

---

[96] Ibid., p. 69.

[97] Ibid., p. 70.

[98] Ibid., pp. 69–70.

[99] *Münâzarât*, p. 31.

[100] Nursi, B. S., *The Rays*, The Fourteenth Ray, p. 401 (translation by Ş. Vahide), accessed September 29, 2014, www.dur.ac.uk/resources/sgia/imeis/14Ray07.pdf.

to us? Why does it not come as a whole?" as follows: *"Only 10 percent of it has been able to come to you. For, poor constitutionalism is afraid of your wild bears, ignorant dragons and hostile wolves dwelling in your savage, ignorant, hostile and steep mountains and streams. If you act lazily and do not pave the way for it, you will be able to see it in one hundred years. For, the distance between you and Istanbul is a month but the distance between you and constitutionalism is more than one thousand months."*[101] That is, permanent change can only be possible through people changing themselves; and the level of democracy in a country is directly proportional to the democracy understanding of the people in that country.

---

[101] *Münâzarât*, p. 29.

Chapter 4

Laicism and Laic Republic

Nursi has always approached matters as a true realist. He read the time and the changing circumstances correctly, and based his movements on real time and space, not illusion. Instead of standing against the winds of republicanism, freedom of religion and conscience, and democracy that blew strongly in the first half of the twentieth century, he regarded these currents as the rising values of the time, and attributed them to the Qur'an.

Nursi demonstrates through *jifr* and *abjad* (numerical symbolism) reckoning that the Qur'anic verse, "*There is no compulsion in religion; truth stands out clear from falsehood, so does belief from infidelity*" (al-Baqarah 2:256) points to our time, and he interprets it as follows: "*The matters of religion being separated from worldly matters on that date, freedom of conscience, which opposes to force and compulsion in religion and to religious struggle and armed jihad for religion, becomes a fundamental law and political principle in governments, and the government turns into 'secular republic.' In view of this, jihad will be a non-physical religious jihad with the sword of certain, verified belief.*"[102]

With this explanation, Nursi presents the freedom of conscience as the most fundamental right and freedom for the people of our time that will be practiced as a universal constitutional principle and a political criterion. He also views the freedom of conscience that prohibits any compulsion and use of force in religion as a natural outcome of the

---

[102] Nursi, B. S., *The Rays*, The Eleventh Ray, p. 290 (translation by Ş. Vahide), accessed September 29, 2014, www.dur.ac.uk/resources/sgia/imeis/7-11Rays07.pdf.

religion. With the expression above, Nursi states that the period of 'ikrah' and 'ijbar' that is, 'the use of force and compulsion' in religion is over, and expresses that all struggles from now on will take place on the common ground of 'freedom of conscience.'

Nursi adds, *"Risale-i Nur's immaterial sword has solved hundreds of the mysteries of religion, leaving no need for physical swords,"*[103] stating that spiritual jihad based on evidence and persuasion will replace material jihad based on power. Therefore, *"Risale-i Nur students do not interfere in the politics and political currents of the world and their material struggles, nor attach importance to them, nor condescend to any involvement with them."*[104] A true Nur student does not feel anger at his most fearsome opponent and cruel enemy, *"but pities and shows compassion to him and tries to reform them, in the hope they shall be saved."*[105]

Nursi stresses that the time for coercion, intimidation, and deception is over, and points out that any change set off by these means by canceling reason and oppressing the conscience is bound to be limited, superficial, and temporary. He expresses that lasting change can only be achieved by the penetration of real truths into the depths of the hearts with the light of sciences, the mobilization of all emotions and abilities, the establishment of high morality, and the preservation of freedom of expression: *"Yes, it is possible to affect and route public opinion into another channel by threats, intimidation, and deception. But its influence would be limited, superficial, and temporary. It might even cancel reason in a short period. But penetrating into the depths of the hearts by its teaching, moving the most delicate emotions, opening the way to the development of abilities, establishing high morals and eliminating and eradicating low character, displaying its truth by unveiling the essence of humanity, and establishing freedom of expression can only be an extraordinary miracle extracted from the rays of truth."*[106]

It is rather ironic that even though Nursi, in opposition to many of his contemporaries, regarded and presented the secular republic as a

---

[103] Ibid.
[104] Ibid.
[105] Ibid.
[106] *İşârâtü'l-İ'câz*, p. 111.

reality of time and was a leading advocate of constitutionalism, republicanism, and constitutional order since childhood, he was taken to courts
and prisons with the exact opposite charges. In fact, in one of his defens-
es, he addressed the attorney general and the judges of the court as
follows: "*You are accusing me of holding an idea opposite to that which
I have held for fifty years. If you ask me about the secular republic, what
I understand by it is that 'secular' (laic) means to be impartial; that is, a
government which, in accordance with the principle of freedom of conscience, does not interfere with the religiously minded and pious, the same
as it does not interfere with the irreligious and dissipated.*"[107] With these
statements, Nursi describes true secularism, and stresses that a secular state, in a modern sense, ought to keep the same distance with both
religious and irreligious people in an impartial way.

In his defense at Eskisehir Court in 1935, Nursi pointed out that a
secular republic should be unbiased and pro-freedom, and demanded
that the government abstain from any practices that disregard freedom of conscience: "*Since the Government of the Republic has accepted
the principle of 'separating religion from worldly matters and not taking
sides,' it is the requisite of this principle to not interfere with religious people for their piety, as it does not interfere with irreligious people for their
irreligion. In this regard, I demand for the Government of the Republic,
which is supposed to be impartial and supportive of freedoms, be disso-
ciated and distanced from the secret corrupt committees that promote
irreligion, plot schemes, and delude government officials with deception;
my struggle is with those scheme plotters.*"[108]

Nursi has always been an advocate of freedom of religion and belief.
He opposes aggression toward irreligious people in the name of religion
as he opposes aggression toward religious people on behalf of irreligion. He even used the principle of freedom of conscience as a basis in
his movement, and rejected any claims that he is against the freedom
of conscience: "*Moreover, freedom of conscience, which is one of the principles of the Government of the Republic that we have most relied on and*

---

[107] Nursi, B. S., *The Rays*, The Fourteenth Ray, p. 379 (translation by Ş. Vahide), accessed September 29, 2014, www.dur.ac.uk/resources/sgia/imeis/14Ray07.pdf.
[108] *Tarihçe-i Hayat*, p. 233.

defended ourselves with, has been made the basis of charges against us as though we oppose the principle of freedom of conscience."[109]

Nursi went even further and labeled the violation of the freedom of conscience as injustice, and violators as aggressors, and stated that the government should stand firm against any attempts to restrict freedoms: "*The Government of the Republic should take the position of a referee between us and the destructors or slayers. Based on who among us is the aggressor and oppresses others, let the judge pass a judgment and enforce its verdict.*"[110]

According to Nursi, "*irreligiousness and religiousness have continued to exist in the universe since the time of Adam and will continue till the Day of Judgment.*"[111] Therefore, the struggle between these two main movements is quite natural. What matters is the practice of this struggle on a free platform and in a civilized way without pressure, threats and force: "*In respect of religion, the civilized are to be conquered through persuasion, not through force, and through showing by conforming to its commands in actions and conduct that Islam is elevated and lovable. Force and enmity are only to combat the barbarity of savages.*"[112]

According to Nursi, the state should not be a party in this struggle. If it is necessary, it should be the religious side, not the irreligious one. For, "*In Asia, the religious movement is dominant. This republican government, which is the forward commander of Asia, will benefit from its natural property and mine. It will use the principle of impartiality in favor of religiousness not irreligiousness.*"[113] As a matter of fact, even in modern Western states where laicism is practiced in its real sense like the USA, the state helps religious institutions indirectly by offering them tax advantages; it also makes all kinds of religious activities easy and encourages religiousness as long as it does not spoil the peace in the community. For sincere religious people are useful for the community and humanity.

---

[109] Ibid., p. 393.
[110] Ibid., p. 234.
[111] Ibid.
[112] *Hutbe-i Şâmiye*, p. 95.
[113] *Tarihçe-i Hayat*, p. 234.

Nursi's lifelong fight was not against secularism, but irreligion and attempts to interpret secularism as irreligion, and he fought against irreligion in the most civilized way—with books on the platform of ideas. This is because ideas can be fought with ideas. His acquittal from all charges of opposing freedom of conscience and laicism at courts of law is proof of this. Nursi expresses that the freedom of conscience that is guaranteed in true secularism is one of the most fundamental principles of this age of freedoms, and he viewed the violation of the freedom of conscience or even the downplaying of its importance as an insult to humanity: *"On what force do you rely that you are so bold as to violate the principle of 'freedom of conscience,' which governs almost everywhere in mankind, especially in this age of freedom and in civilized circles, and to treat it lightly and so indirectly to insult mankind and dismiss their objections? What power do you have that you attack religion and the people of religion in this way as though you had taken irreligion as a religion for yourselves in bigoted fashion, although by calling yourselves 'secular' you proclaim that you will interfere with neither religion nor irreligion? Such a thing will not remain secret!"*[114]

Nursi's life is full of examples of struggle against the application of laicism in the form of enmity of religion in a way that eliminates freedom of conscience. For instance, the printing of his book called *Gençlik Rehberi* (A Guide for Youth), which is full of useful advice and recommendations for youth in order to make them attain happiness in the hereafter and which has nothing to do with politics, was regarded as contrary to laicism in 1952 and he was sued. In his petition presented to the criminal court, attraction is drawn to the fact that laicism is freedom of conscience and thought, and answers to the following questions are demanded: *"What is the meaning of laicism if Gençlik Rehberi is accused of being contrary to laicism because it gives religious education? We ask: Is laicism enmity against Islam? Is laicism freedom of attacking religion for those who assume irreligiousness as their religion? Is laicism a principle of absolute despotism that locks the mouths and handcuffs the hands*

---

[114] Nursi, B. S., *The Letters*, The Twenty-Ninth Letter, p. 493 (translation by Ş. Vahide), accessed September 29, 2014, www.dur.ac.uk/resources/sgia/imeis/Lets29_2_SofR.pdf.

of those who express the truths of religion and give Islamic lessons?"[115] The court acquitted him; thus, it is recorded that laicism is not enmity against religion.

Although he was repeatedly accused of being a reactionary, it can be easily seen through his works that Nursi indeed was a great ideologue and a true revolutionary. He rode horses on the territories of ideas untouched by even the imagination of others. He also boldly expressed ideas on most unwelcoming platforms on which many would not dare to speak. And most importantly, he did all these things by walking a straight line with no zigzags all his life. Nursi evaluated everything within the realities of the time, and on the ground of reason.

To give an example, he gave the following response to the flurries of people who asked him during the time of constitutionalism how Armenians and other non-Muslims could be mayors and governors: *"Just like they can become watchmakers, mechanics, and broom makers. This is because constitutionalism is the sovereignty of people. Government is a servant. If the constitutionalism is established right, mayors and governors are not chiefs; rather, they are just paid civil servants. A non-Muslim cannot be a chief, but can be a civil servant."*[116] Here, what is described by the name 'constitutionalism' is in fact republicanism under which the public or the people are masters and the officials are servants. Even in circumstances with underdeveloped democracy, Nursi supports non-Muslims to hold governorships and other high administrative positions, and he justifies this stand on the basis of reason and logic: *"Suppose that a high official post is a sort of presidency and aghahood (tribal leadership). When we share power with three thousand non-Muslims in presidency and leadership, the road opens for the presidency of three hundred thousand men from the nation of Islam all around the world. One who loses one but wins a thousand is not at a loss."*[117] The statement above is a comprehensive and extremely rational angle of view that is broad enough to include the present as well as the future, and

---

[115] *Emirdağ Lahikası-2*, p. 127.
[116] *Münâzarât*, p. 40.
[117] Ibid.

the country as well as the world. It is also an indication that Nursi's statements are universal and timeless.

To those who objected to the governorship of non-Muslims because some duties of governors are associated with the laws of sharia, Nursi gave the following inspirational response: *"Henceforth the office of religious affairs representing the Caliphate and the post of sheikhulislam will necessarily be exalted, sacred, separate, and overseer."*[118] It is as if Nursi has seen the future with his deep probing eyesight and stated that from then on, religious and state affairs will necessarily be separated. The position of the religious affairs office will rise in the eyes of people and, by protecting its sacredness, will be more effective on consciences since it will be outside political influences.

In fact, these statements are in conformity with the modern democratic administration, in which the individual is put in the center instead of the state and in which the individuals do not exist for the state but the state exists to serve the individuals. Religious orders and prohibitions will always exist. However, the state will not apply them by force; individuals will apply them themselves. That is, religion will live through the free wills of individuals, not through the pressure of the state authority. It will be supervised by religious communities as non-governmental organizations. The state will represent the common ground of the community, will prioritize the highest social interests, and will provide the highest right to live for all kinds of lifestyles. For, people who ended the period of childhood and have entered the period of adulthood cannot be treated like children.

Since the beginning of the 1900s, Nursi stated that the institution of the Caliphate, which is represented by an individual, has completed its time. He suggested that in order to be attuned to the values of the time in which democracy and public opinion rule, this institution too needs to represent a *"collective personality that is composed of a council of distinguished scholars,"*[119] representing not only the Ottomans, but the entire Muslim world: *"Time has shown that the office of religious*

---

[118] Ibid.

[119] *Sünûhât*, p. 33.

affairs, the post of sheikhulislam, representing the Caliphate does not belong to Istanbul and Ottomans alone. It is an exalted institution that comprises the entire Muslim world. However, with the faded position it is in now, it is not even adequate to guide just Istanbul, let alone the entire Muslim world. Therefore, this position should be transformed into such a form that the Muslim world can trust it. It should serve the position of both a source and a mirror, and it should perform its religious duty rightfully to the Muslim world."[120] Such an institution representing the common denominator among Muslims living in dozens of countries will necessarily stay out of politics and will not form any organic ties with any political movement—just like the papacy in Rome, which represents the religious authority of the all Catholics in the world and expresses their feelings by shedding light on them.

By pointing out that public opinion rules in this time, Nursi expressed the opinion that religious affairs also should be conducted not by an individual, but by a council representing the public opinion of the Islamic World: *"Now that the ruler is the public opinion, and not an individual, the same kind of jurisprudence is required."*[121] Nursi also mentions that in the establishment of such a council *"about fifteen to twenty distinguished religious scholars for now are needed from the Islamic World outside who have gained the trust of Islam in terms of piety and morality."*[122] Such a council would serve as a 'Religious Affairs High Consultation Council' for the Muslim world. It would play an effective and constructive role in ending the current conflict of ideas in the Muslim world and forming a consensus. And it will do all this without shaking the secular nature of any state and without violating any individual's freedom of conscience.

---

[120] Ibid.

[121] *Münâzarât*, p. 40.

[122] *Sünûhât*, p. 35.

Chapter 5

Sharia, Despotism, and Intellect

O f the concepts that are misunderstood the most in this age of information and are known by the opposite of what they are, probably Islam and sharia come among the first. Islam, which is in fact a religion of peace, security, justice and love, has been virtually identified with terror; especially in the West, it is remembered as a religion of fighting, enmity, bullying, and hatred. The Qur'an regards killing an innocent person as equal to killing all people as it is stated in the following verse: "*if anyone slew a person—unless it be for murder or for spreading mischief in the land—it would be as if he slew the whole people*" (al-Maeda 5:32). Nursi interprets this verse as follows: "*The life and blood of a person cannot be sacrificed even for the whole of humanity. They are the same in terms of the endless power of Allah and in terms of justice.*"[123] The Prophet of Islam defines a Muslim as "a person who does not harm people through his tongue and hands." Then, it is not possible for terror, which causes the death of many innocent people by targeting civilians and spreads horror and fear among people, to comply with Islam. However, those who deal with the issue superficially have identified terror with Islam by looking at the identity of the terrorists, settled the image of "Islamic terrorist" in the minds and caused one and a half billion Muslims to be seen as terrorists. The term "Islamophobia," which implies that Islam is a religion that intimidates people, strengthened this image. The first thing to do in order to eliminate this image, which was formed by evil-minded people and some Mus-

---

[123] *Sünûhât*, p. 11.

lims, is to draw the true image clearly with consensus and inform people about this image.

Similarly, when sharia is mentioned, what comes to mind first are repulsive images such as oppression, tyranny, prohibition, despotism, anti-freedom, incompatibility with democracy and republicanism, discord with modern life, deprivation from all kinds of freedom, including the freedoms of conscience and expression, intolerance, fear, anger, violence, clergy-centered governing, disregarding public opinion, using religious formalism as the source and reasoning of laws and their applications, making fatwa from clergy an essential source of decision-making, avoiding the realities of time and even declaring war against them, pushing intellect into the background and even eliminating it, opposing sciences, having bigotry and prejudice rule the society, and finally, matching with the term "backwardness," driving society back into the dark ages of the past. This definition has nothing to do with the real sharia, which is the collection of religious commands and prohibitions. In fact, the description above is completely opposite to Islam and the real sharia. Unfortunately, this wrong image is reinforced by some despotic regimes that present bigotry, fanaticism, and enmity as sharia and by some religious functionaries who need to enlighten the community but who themselves are stuck in bigotry and darkness of doubts.

Nursi's understanding of sharia has nothing to do with the frightful and fallacious description above. He put some distance between himself and these kinds of wrong understandings, and explained the real nature of sharia, which is identical with Islam and the Qur'an, on every occasion. He never made any concessions about it. As a matter of fact, he played an important role in the incident known as backwardness revolt on March 31, 1909, and soothed the revolt through his effective speeches by preventing many people from taking part in the revolt, but even so, he was sent to the military court and capital punishment was demanded for him. In an environment where the dead bodies of about fifteen religious scholars could be seen hanging, the chief justice of the court said to Nursi, "You also wanted sharia. Is that right?" Nursi answered him recklessly as follows: "*For one truth of sharia, I am ready to sacrifice if I have one thousand spirits. For, sharia is the cause of hap-*

*piness, pure justice and virtue. However, it is not like what the revolution-
ists want.*"[124] In this defense, which ended in acquittal though people
expected execution, Nursi defined sharia as pure justice, the highest
humanity and a means of happiness.

First of all, it is necessary to state that the addressee of religion is the
individual, and not the state, and this can be seen clearly in Qur'an's
expressions. Therefore, sharia actually is a guide and a handbook that
consists of the necessary rules to be followed for those who wish to
live their lives in accordance with their beliefs. And these rules are to
be followed freely; not to be imposed on others and force them to follow.
It will be seen that this is even more so when viewed from the window
of the principles of the freedom of conscience and the separation of religious and state affairs, which are the fundamental values of our time,
in the light of the Qur'anic verse, "there is no compulsion in religion,"
explained beforehand.

In conclusion, even the sincere religious people experience a dilemma due to this contradiction in terms and they regard religion and sharia as different things justifiably. For instance, according to a research
made by TESEV in 2006, 93 percent of the people in Turkey regard themselves as somewhat religious, but the rate of those who want a religious state based on sharia is only 9 percent.[125] Similarly, according to
the survey made by Gallup, whose central office is in New York, in ten
Muslim countries in 2005 and 2006, 86 percent of Turks stated that
religion had a very important place in their daily lives, but the rate of
those who wanted sharia in their country was only 9 percent—that is,
only one in ten.[126] According to a survey made in 2009 by Sabancı University, the rate of those who believed in Allah and the hereafter was
93 percent but the rate of those who wanted sharia was 10 percent.[127]

In Turkey today, the word sharia has become a taboo due to the
negative images it brings to mind; it was virtually driven out of the
religion by being covered by a black cloth. In the Western world, Islam

---

[124] *Dîvân-ı Harb-i Örfî*, p. 19; *Tarihçe-i Hayat*, p. 57.
[125] *Sabah* and *Yeni Şafak* newspapers, 22 November 2006.
[126] *Hürriyet* newspaper, 23 February 2007.
[127] *Radikal* newspaper, 18 Kasım 2009.

has been identified with terror, and sharia has been identified with opposition to democracy and republic; religiousness, which has been stigmatized as backwardness, has been seen as a potential threat and danger for the laic republic. These perversions are important since they show that ideas are formed instead of true knowledge on the ground of ignorance.

In Turkey, religious scholars and functionaries avoid talking about and mentioning sharia, but Nursi is quite relaxed when he uses this word. He uses it without being apologetic. Nursi described the four fundamental principles of sharia as ethics (morals), worship, afterlife, and virtue, all of which fall under the category of freedom of conscience and have nothing to do with politics or state affairs, and refers the small fraction associated with politics to the understanding of politicians: *"Ninety-nine percent of sharia consists of ethics, worship, afterlife, and virtue. Just one percent is related to politics; and we let our rulers think about that part."*[128] That is, in a truly secular state where freedom of conscience exist in essence, not just in words, a pious Muslim can live 99 percent of his religion or sharia without being concerned with politics and government, and he can do so without causing any uneasiness or posing a threat. As for the remaining 1 percent concerning politics and state affairs, it is sufficient to use reason and sciences as the basis for governing in accordance with the practice of modern states, and this approach is perfectly compatible with sharia. Because for Nursi, *"sharia consists of rational laws."*[129]

Besides, a right mind and a rightly understood *naql*, religious resource or narration, cannot contradict one another since their source is the same: *"This is such a sharia that by the alliance and joining of aql and naql (reason and narration) hand in hand, have confirmed the validity of the truth of the sharia."*[130] If there appears to be a contradiction, reason is taken as the base: *"It is among the established methods of usul, Islamic sciences and jurisprudence, that if aql, reason, and naql, narration contradict one another, reason is taken as the base while religion is inter-*

---

[128] *Tarihçe-i Hayat*, p. 64.
[129] *Mesnevî-i Nuriye*, p. 232.
[130] *Muhâkemât*, p. 3.

preted. But, that reason should truly be reason."[131] This is because reason is a valid criterion and a uniting reference for all humankind, and Islam cannot be understood or applied in a way that common sense cannot accept. The mind's inability and weakness to understand is something and being unreasonable or illogical is something else.

Nursi regards acting upon evidence by using the intellect and reasoning as part of the real Islam based on the Qur'an and rejects imitating religions scholars blindly. He goes further and regards the domination of the intellect, science, and knowledge as the domination of the Qur'an: "*We Muslims, who are students of the Qur'an, follow proof; we approach the truths of belief through reason, though, and our hearts. We do not abandon proof in favor of blind obedience and imitation of the clergy like some adherents of other religions. Therefore, in the future, when the intellect, science, and technology prevail, of a certainty, that will be the time the Qur'an will gain ascendancy, which relies on rational proofs and invites the intellect to confirm its pronounce.*"[132] Nursi predicts that the Qur'anic approach and the intellectual and scientific approach will unite at the same point in the future though their starting points are different. That is, the intellect will discover the Qur'an.

Nursi says there cannot be a contradiction between the religion and the rational and scientific facts and describes the following statement as a foolish saying: "*This is opposed to the religion, even though it is an established fact.*" He even doubts their intellect: "*Anyone who deems it probable that something which has been uncontrovertibly established can be opposed to the Religion, which is itself an embodiment of pure truth and accommodates every truth is not sane.*"[133] That is, to think that an established fact like the roundness of the world and its rotation around the sun does not comply with the religion is a sign of foolishness.

While some view Islam as a threat to humanity and sharia as a menace to civilization, Nursi exclaims just the opposite. For him, "*Islam is the greatest humanness, and sharia is the most virtuous civilization; and therefore, the Muslim world is worthy of being the virtuous civilization of*

---

[131] Ibid., p. 9.
[132] *Hutbe-i Şâmiye*, p. 26.
[133] *Muhâkemât*, p. 42.

Plato."[134] Nursi defines sharia as absolute justice and virtue: *"Sharia is the source of happiness, absolute justice, and virtue."*[135] The outcome of justice and righteousness is happiness. Therefore, oppression and sharia never comply with each other.

Along with the sharia that we know and that arranges the deeds of people, Nursi mentions another sharia known as the laws of creation dominating the acts of matter in nature: *"Allah has two kinds of sharia. One issues from the Divine Attribute of Speech and regulates or orders the acts of servants issuing from their free will. The other issues from the Divine Attribute of Will, comprises the Divine commands of creation, and is the result of the Divine way of acting. The first one comprises comprehensible laws, while the second one consists of nominal laws, wrongly called 'laws of nature.'"*[136] That is, the sharia we know consists of comprehensible laws and nature consists of scientific laws like the laws of physics.

Nursi states that the punishment for opposing the religious orders are generally inflicted in the hereafter and punishment for acting contrarily to the laws and principles of the world are generally inflicted in the world: *"Just as there is obedience and rebellion in the face of the commands of the sharia, so too there is obedience and rebellion in the face of the creative commands in the universe. With regard to the first, the reward and punishment are mostly in the hereafter, while with the second, they are mostly in this world. For example, the reward of patience is victory; the punishment for idleness is poverty; the reward of effort is wealth, and the reward of constancy, triumph. Justice without equality is not justice."*[137]

The notion that sharia is not compatible with republicanism is a complete fallacy, and the fact that the regime during the earliest days of Islam was a republic based on public opinion is an evidence of such. Moreover, public opinion has always been a valid source of decision-making in Islam: *"As consensus and public opinion have always been a source of fatwa (ruling) according to the Luminous Sharia, now there is*

---

[134] *Tarihçe-i Hayat*, p. 71.
[135] Ibid., p. 57.
[136] *Mesnevî-i Nuriye*, p. 232.
[137] *Mektubat*, pp. 536–537.

a vital need for a similar decision due to the conflict of opinions." [138] Nursi regards caliphate not as an indivisible part of sultanate but as something opposite to it; he regards the Siffin War as a struggle between caliphate and sultanate: *"When it comes to Imam Ali's war with Mu'awiya at Siffin, that was a war over the caliphate and rule. That is to say, taking the injunctions of religion, the truths of Islam, and the Hereafter as the basis, Imam Ali, may God be pleased with him, sacrificed some of the laws of government and pitiless demands of politics to them."* [139] Nursi regards the struggle between Hasan and Husayn and Umayyads as a war between religion and nationalism.

Nursi, who advocated freedoms and true democracy throughout his life and thus often differed from his contemporaries, does not initiate a reform in religion; rather, he is trying to unveil the youthful and bright essence of the religion by stripping it of formalism and cleaning the mud masking its beauty. In fact, he screams like his body is on fire because of the nation's backwardness, and cries out in regret: *"We have abandoned the essence of Islam and concentrated instead on its shell; in doing so, we have deceived ourselves. Having committed mistakes and fallen short of the ethical standards we should have had, we have failed to give Islam its due and the respect it deserves. As a result, it has recoiled from us in disgust, hiding itself in the miasma of whims and suppositions that we have formed around it."* [140]

In modern states, governing is based on reason and science. It is interesting that Nursi bases the sharia, which some people think rejects reason and science, on the same firm ground. He goes even further and states that sharia is distilled from information and sciences: *"Sharia of Islam is established on the basis of rational proof. This sharia is extracted from the sciences and branches of knowledge that encompass the vital points of the fundamental sciences."* [141] In addition, he expressed that sharia only laid the fundamental principles like justice and virtue,

---

[138] *Sünûhât*, p. 34.
[139] Nursi, B. S., *The Letters*, The Fifteenth Letter, p. 493 (translation by Ş. Vahide), accessed September 29, 2014, www.dur.ac.uk/resources/sgia/imeis/Lets15-18.pdf.
[140] *Muhâkemât*, p. 4.
[141] *İşârâtü'l-İ'câz*, p. 114.

and left extracting laws from these principles and the details to reason and consultation, to be done in accordance with the requirements of time and place: "*It laid down the principles, but referred the rules to be extracted from those principles or the secondary matters to be resolved to the consultation of the minds.*"[142] That is, he attracts attention to the kernel, not the shell. For this reason, Nursi has supported the first constitution, which was declared during the reign of Sultan Abdulhamid in the name of religion, while others opposed in the same name.

In response to the question about constitutionalism (republicanism), "Some say that it is 'contrary to Sharia,'" Nursi stated that the essence of republicanism is from sharia, but there can be deviations in application: "*The spirit of constitutionalism is from sharia, so is its life. However, there can be some details that temporarily appear to be contradictory due to the requirements of the circumstances.*"[143] He goes on, by portraying a realistic approach, and reminds that not a single thing or person or government can be in 100 percent compliance with sharia, and invites all to become realistic: "*And yet, what thing is there that is compatible with sharia in all aspects? What person is there whose behaviors are perfectly attuned with sharia? This being the case, a government, which is a collective personality, cannot be innocent either; except in the imaginary city of virtue that Plato defined in his philosophy. Nevertheless, the roads of abuse are blocked in constitutionalism; but they are open in despotism.*"[144] Nursi again proves his argument by using logic and rationale, and expresses that while constitutionalism (republicanism) is closed to abuse to a large extent, its alternative, despotism, is quite open to abuse, and thus despotism is totally contrary to sharia, whose core values are justice and virtue.

However, an individual is vulnerable to outside effects, but the parliament is resistant. "*The wind can move a thin wire as it wishes. However, the unbreakable rope formed by union will not be affected by the*

---

[142] Ibid.

[143] *Münâzarât*, p. 38.

[144] Ibid., p. 39.

strongest things . . . The will of the previous sultans could be veered by the Armenian wind and the foreign chiefs or the delusions."[145]

Nursi expresses that in sharia, general societal agreement constitutes a valid base, public opinion forms a foundation, and the general public inclination is a valid criterion in decision-making. "*Consensus of society is strong evidence in sharia. Public opinion is a basis in sharia. The general inclination of the society is cherished and respected in sharia.*"[146] Thus, "*The majority of people should be followed.*"[147] Nursi states that in a properly working democracy, a council of three hundred representatives can agree only on what is right and beneficial for the society, and this would be perfectly compatible with sharia: "*Three hundred disagreeing votes and differing opinions would not agree on anything other than what is right and beneficial, or they would not keep quiet. Righteousness and benefit are fundamentals in sharia.*"[148]

Nursi puts emphasis on the requirements of time as well, and points out that something known as haram (prohibited) can turn into its opposite and become *wajib* (necessary) by the forcing of circumstances: "*However, by the principle of sharia 'Necessities render prohibitions permitted,' something we know as haram, prohibited, could sometimes become wajib, required by the force of necessities. A rotting finger is cut in order to save the hand. If the safety of a nation necessitates the essence of life, it would be sacrificed with no hesitation; as has been done in the past.*"[149]

Nursi also mentions that sharia can change with regards to time and place and even to the nature of communities: "*Yes, just as clothes change with the change of the seasons, and medicines change according to dispositions, so sacred laws change according to the ages, and their ordinances change according to the capacities of people. Because the*

---

[145] Ibid., p. 40.

[146] Ibid.

[147] *Mektubat* p. 534.

[148] *Münâzarât*, p. 40.

[149] Ibid.

*secondary matters of the ordinances of the sharia look to human cir-
cumstances, they come according to them, and are like medicine.*"[150]

In this context, Nursi mentions the importance of dealing with
issues carefully by acting with balance and taking the conditions of
time into consideration; he also warns people against memorizers and
formalists: "*Those who want sharia are divided into two: one group wants
to apply constitutionalism to sharia carefully by taking balance and necessities into consideration. The other group deviates into a blind alley without any balance and by giving importance to outside appearance.*"[151]

It can be said in the light of the arguments above that decisions made
and laws passed by a parliament that consists of at least three hundred deputies on the basis of reason, science, common good, and the
realities of the time in a democratic environment are entirely compatible with sharia. Indeed, Nursi states that anything contradicting a truth
of sharia would also be contradictory of republic as well. Even when
this may not be the case, he does not see it as an issue worth quarrel-
ing about, since he thinks only one thousandth of sharia is concerned
with politics: "*In my view, matters that are contrary to the truth of sharia are also contrary to constitutionalism as well. They are either its sins
or the coercion of the circumstances. Just assume that the current politics are contrary to sharia; still, there is no need for concern since it is
only one thousandth of the Luminous Sharia that is related to politics. By
neglecting that part, sharia is not neglected. Yes, not adhering does not
mean denying.*"[152]

Nursi finds the presence of non-Muslim minorities in the parliament as deputies quite acceptable. He answered the question, "*There
are Christians and Jews in the National Assembly; what importance do
their views have in sharia?*" as follows, by emphasizing the importance
of competence and upholding the law: "*First of all, in mutual consultation, the majority opinion rules. The majority is Muslim, composed of over*

---

[150] Nursi, B. S., *The Words*, The Twenty-Seventh Word, p. 500 (translation by Ş. Vahide), accessed September 29, 2014, www.dur.ac.uk/resources/sgia/imeis/words2627_07_.pdf.

[151] *Münâzarât*, p. 40.

[152] Ibid., p. 39.

sixty ulama (scholars). Deputies are free; they should not be under any influence. That means Islam rules. Secondly, in making watches or operating machines, the opinions of the craftsman Hacho and the operator Behram count. As sharia does not reject this, the political benefits and wisdom as well as economic benefits in the National Assembly are mostly of this kind, and should not be rejected either. The fundamental laws, judgments, and rights are not subject to change at all; they are the applications and preferences that necessitate consultation. The duty of deputies is to not abuse those fundamental laws, judgments, and rights, and to pass some laws and to build a great wall around them in order to prevent any deception and abuse by some clergy and judges."[153]

As mentioned earlier, "*the source of Islam is knowledge (al-'ilm) and its basis is reason (al-'aql).*"[154] Therefore, it can be said that regimes based on reason, science, and consultation within the framework of the freedom of speech and expression and have the backing of the general public are fully compatible with Islam together with the laws and regulations associated with the regimes so long as basic codes of morality such as justice and virtue are observed. Further, it can be said that even if such regimes are not the same as the 1 percent, part of sharia dealing with politics and government, they are not different from it either. When the realities of time such as 'there is no compulsion in religion' and 'the true ruler is public opinion and the government is a servant' are considered, it can be said that the democratic regimes that observe the basic human rights and freedoms and uphold justice and law are totally compatible with sharia even if they do not seem to take religion as a reference. This is because relying on reason, science, and public opinion in governments in these modern times is relying on Islam.

This does not mean that religious and moral values, such as abstaining from lying and bribery, will be completely left out of politics and governing. It only means that such values can be incorporated after being adopted as universal or moral values after being filtered through common sense, reason, science, and conscience. In fact, this code of universal moral values is becoming like a common "religion" of the world,

---

[153]   Ibid., p. 41.
[154]   *İşârâtü'l-İ'câz*, p. 105.

and, with values originating from religion, this code fills the moral and spiritual gap that occurred as the religion took the back stage in public life during the secularization period. For instance, the basis of Islam in regards to political matters is justice and virtue. But the whole world can agree to accept these values, which are universal values, as basis in mutual relationships. However, even though the outcome may be the same, it is difficult to have an agreement on accepting religious values as basis even in a single country, let alone the entire world. Nursi's statement, *"Truths do not change by the change of their names"*[155] sheds enough light on to this matter.

Likewise, when explaining why Daru'l-Hikmati'l-Islamiyya, the Religious Affairs Department, was dysfunctional during the late phase of the Ottomans, Nursi makes the following universal remark that opens the minds: *"One might lose the right while going after the most right. Since there is unity in the right, but disunity in the most right; often the right is more right than the most right. During the period of search for the most right, tolerating the presence of fallacy is acceptable. Sometimes beautiful is more beautiful than the most beautiful."*[156] That is, good is often better than the best since there is a unity in good but disunity in the best. The rise and shine of humanity intellectually and morally to reach perfection requires a phase of development, and it is a matter time. Here is the difference that shows when examining events with the mind lit up and the reason grinding. Here is the Nursi difference.

---

[155] *Tarihçe-i Hayat*, p. 70.
[156] *Sünûhât*, p. 89.

Chapter 6

Religion, Politics, and Political Islam

I n his writings, Nursi has always considered life in the hereafter together with life on this earth, and placed eternal afterlife at the center rather than temporary earthly life. To him, the earth is a guesthouse for humanity, while the hereafter is a real homeland. The earth is a testing ground, while the hereafter is a place of reward or punishment. The importance of the world is due to its being the preparation field of the afterlife. The primary goal of religion is to provide for the hereafter rather than administering worldly matters. The key to eternal happiness in the hereafter is belief. Therefore, Nursi sees belief as the most important matter for humankind, and unbelief that threatens eternal life as the greatest danger facing humanity. To him, saving one's belief is like saving an eternal world, and this is more important than gaining ownership of this entire temporary world. As a result, Nursi dedicated most of his life to serving faith, and devoted it to saving belief. He viewed service to faith that manifested itself as books in the *Risale-i Nur* collection above all worldly politics. Nursi states that *Risale-i Nur* earns *"every individual whose belief is under danger a dominion and a triumph that is more beneficial than the dominion of this entire world."* He also points out that gaining belief is more important than gaining the dominion of this world: *"Yes, an individual's belief is the key and the light of an eternal property as wide as this world."*[157]

---

[157] *Kastamonu Lahikası*, p. 18.

After starting to write *Risale-i Nur*, Nursi ran away from politics as he would run away from Satan in order to preclude the rise of even the tiniest doubt about using religion for political gain. To reflect this sentiment, he often used the expression, "*I seek refuge with God from Satan and from politics.*"[158] To support his words with action, he did not show even the smallest interest in the greatest political events, including World War II. When asked the following question about the World War II: "*For fifty days now—and now seven years have passed—you have asked nothing at all about this ghastly World War, which has plunged the whole world into chaos and is closely connected with the fate of the Islamic world, nor have you been curious about it. . . . Is there some event more momentous than the war?*" He replied as follows:

"*Yes, an event more momentous than this World War and a case more important than that of world supremacy has been opened over the heads of everyone and especially Muslims, so that if everyone had the wealth and power of the Germans and English and sense as well, they would unhesitatingly spend all of it to win that single case. The case is this: relying on the thousands of promises and pledges of the universe's Owner, who has disposal over it, hundreds, thousands of the most eminent of mankind, and uncounted numbers of its stars and guides, have unanimously given news—and some of them have actually seen—that for everyone the case has opened by which they may either win, in return for belief, or lose, eternal properties as broad as the earth set with palaces and gardens. If they do not secure the document of belief, they will lose. And in this age, many are losing the case because of the plague of materialism. One of the diviners of reality and investigators of truth observed in one place that out of forty people who died, only a few won; the others lost. Can anything take the place of that lost suit, even ruling over the whole world?*"[159]

Nursi likened belief to a diamond, and politics and worldly matters to pieces of glass. Therefore, he viewed the use of religion as a tool of

---

[158] Nursi, B. S., *The Letters*, The Thirteenth Letter, p. 67 (translation by Ş. Vahide), accessed September 29, 2014, www.dur.ac.uk/resources/sgia/imeis/Lets1-13.pdf.

[159] Nursi, B. S., *The Rays*, The Eleventh Ray, p. 224 (translation by Ş. Vahide), accessed September 29, 2014, www.dur.ac.uk/resources/sgia/imeis/7-11Rays07.pdf.

politics as an injustice and insult to religion, and lowering of its value in the sight of people. Hence, when asked why the service of Qur'an and belief prohibited him from politics, he responded: *"Since the truths of belief and the Qur'an are each like diamonds, if I was polluted by politics, the ordinary people who are easily deceived would wonder about those diamonds I was holding, 'Aren't they for political propaganda to attract more supporters?!' They might regard the diamonds as bits of common glass. Then by being involved with politics, I would be wrong the diamonds as though reducing their value."* [160]

In the past, religion and politics were embedded; all looks were on the hereafter and the religion had been put on the highest position; therefore, politics and political posts could be used in order to serve the religion. Even sultans regarded themselves as servants of the Qur'an. Said Nursi also tried to serve Islam through politics in his period of life he named as "Old (Previous) Said," but these efforts, which he later described as "useless tiredness," turned out to be unsuccessful due to the changing conditions of the world. Nursi saw that the desire of living a comfortable world life was put in the highest position and that religion was left in the background due to the attractiveness of the wonders of the civilization. As a matter of fact, Nursi explains the verse, *"Those who love the life of this world more than the Hereafter..."* (Ibrahim 14:3) as follows: *"One of the properties of this century is that it makes people prefer the worldly life to the otherworldly life deliberately. That is, it has become a principle to prefer a piece of breakable glass to eternal diamond deliberately."* [161]

In this age and time when all faces are turned to worldly matters, and earthly life is placed in the center while the afterlife is sidestepped, it is unavoidable for religion to be lowered to a political matter and to be used as a support element to politics if religion and politics are mixed. Under current conditions, religion and politics are a deadly combination; such a combination will result in the politicization of the religion, and not the spiritualization of politics, and it did. For example, the phrase

---

[160] Nursi, B. S., *The Letters*, The Sixteenth Letter, p. 82 (translation by Ş. Vahide), accessed September 29, 2014, www.dur.ac.uk/resources/sgia/imeis/Lets15-18.pdf.
[161] *Kastamonu Lahikası*, p. 76.

that resonates in our ears is "political Islam," and not "Islamic politics." It is unfortunate that Islam, which embraces humanity as a whole and offers happiness both in this world and the hereafter, is reduced to a political ideology. Even worse, Islam is used as the raw material in political reactionary movements founded on hatred, enmity, and destruction. This resulted in the association of Islam with these negative acts and images in public opinion globally. This has led many societies to remain distant to Islam, and even to take a hostile position towards it. While Imam al-Ghazali described jihad as removing barriers between people and religion, unfortunately, today this term is used to mean just the opposite, meaning placing barriers between people and religion. The destruction of Islam is confused with serving Islam, and the confusion still continues. It is as though Islam, which belongs to humanity as a whole, is taken hostage by a political faction.

Past experiences show clearly beyond any doubt that religion and politics are a fatal combination in this age, and this should be avoided no matter how pure and well-meaning the intentions are. It can even be said that the door of service to religion through politics is closed. Those who attempt to serve religion via politics harm religion, and drive people further from religion. Nursi, who spent all his life serving the belief of Islam and who regarded saving the belief of even only one person superior to the politics of the whole world, drew attention to that danger and warned those who wanted to go into politics that they should do it on behalf of themselves, not on behalf of the religion or a religious movement:

"Risale-i Nur is beyond all movements in the world and belongs to everybody; therefore, it will not follow anybody and will not be included in anything. Against the irreligious people who violate the rights of others, it will help the group that is right and become their friends; it will be the anchor for them in case of emergency. However, some brothers can go into politics on behalf of themselves, not on behalf of Risale-i Nur in order to spread and avail Risale-i Nur. The blessed Isparta has been the school of Risale-i Nur and its opposers have not disturbed it very much;

if it does not assume a partial attitude in the country, it can cause the opposers to repent and return to the truth."[162]

As is understood from the statement above, Nursi does not want his students to support any political movements, let alone going into politics. For, such a stance may cause those who have opposite views to assume an adversary stance against the service of Islamic belief and prevent them from benefitting from the service of Islamic belief. Nursi does not leave any room for misinterpretation and misunderstanding: *"Beware, my brothers! Do not fancy or imagine that I am urging you with these words to busy yourselves with politics. God forbid! The truth of Islam is above all politics. All politics may serve it, but no politics can make Islam a tool for itself."*[163]

Nursi shows that he is a realist on every occasion and approaches incidents meticulously, like a surgeon. According to him, the biggest illness of the century he lives in is belieflessness, which comes through the channel of science based on materialism and which confuses the mind and harms the heart; the cure for this illness is the explanations and proofs of *Risale-i Nur* based on reason and logic that persuade the mind and satisfy the heart. Nursi states that interventions made by politics through using force—even if they succeed—will cause a reaction; he advises people to cling to the light:

"The greatest danger facing the people of Islam at this time is their hearts being corrupted and belief harmed through the misguidance that arises from science and philosophy. The sole solution for this is light; it is to show light so that their hearts can be reformed and their belief, saved. If one acts with the club of politics and prevails over them, the unbelievers descend to the degree of dissemblers. And dissemblers are worse than unbelievers. That is to say, the club cannot heal the heart at this time, for then unbelief enters the heart and is concealed, and is transformed into dissembling. And at this time, a powerless person like myself cannot employ both of them—the club and the light. For this reason I am compelled to embrace the light with all my strength, and cannot consider the club of

---

[162] *Emirdağ Lahikası*-1, p. 150.
[163] *Hutbe-i Şâmiye*, p. 56.

politics whatever form it is in. Whatever physical jihad demands, we are not charged with that duty at the moment. Yes, in accordance with a person's way, a club is necessary to form a barrier against the assaults of the unbelievers or apostates. But we only have two hands. Even if we had a hundred hands, they would be sufficient only for the light. We do not have any other hands with which to hold the club!"[164]

Nursi states that religion and politics should not be intermingled and that it is necessary to keep away from politics in this century in order to have an effective service of Islamic belief:

"Human life is a journey. I saw at this time through the light of the Qur'an that the way has entered a swamp. The caravan of mankind is stumbling forward in stinking and filthy mud. Part of it is traveling a safe way. Part of it has found certain means to save itself as far as is possible from the muddy swamp. The great majority are traveling, in darkness in the stinking, filthy, muddy swamp. Twenty percent suppose the filthy mud to be musk and ambergris because they are drunk, and are smearing it over their faces and eyes... they stumble on till they drown in it. However, 80 percent understand it is a swamp and realize it is stinking and filthy, but they are bewildered and cannot see the safe way.

"Thus, there are two solutions for these: The First: to bring the drunken 20 percent to their senses with a club. The Second: to point out the safe way to the bewildered by showing them a light.

"I look and see that eighty people are brandishing clubs at the twenty while the light is not shown truly to the unhappy and bewildered eighty. And even if it is shown, since those showing it have both the club and the light in one hand, it does not inspire confidence. The bewildered man anxiously wonders: "Does he want to attract me with the light then hit me with the club?" And sometimes when, due to some defect, the club is broken, the light flies away too or else is extinguished.

"And so, the swamp is the dissolute social life of mankind, which breeds heedlessness and misguidance. The drunkards are those obdurate people who take delight in misguidance, and the bewildered, those who detest

---

[164] *The Flashes*, The Sixteenth Flash, p. 144 (translation by Ş. Vahide), accessed September 29, 2014, www.dur.ac.uk/resources/sgia/imeis/2Fl0981-156.pdf.

misguidance, but cannot extract themselves from it. They want to be saved, but cannot find the way: they are confused. As for the clubs, they are the political currents. And the light, the truths of the Qur'an. Light cannot be disputed, nor can enmity be held towards it. No one can detest it apart from Satan the Accursed.

"And so, in order to hold in my hand the light of the Qur'an, I said, "I seek refuge with God from Satan and from politics," and throwing away the club of politics, embraced the light with both hands. I saw that in the political currents, there are lovers of those lights in both the opposition and the supporters. It is necessary that no side and no group casts aspersions on or holds back from the lights of the Qur'an which are shown, and from the teachings of the Qur'an which are in a position far above all political currents and partisanship, and are exempt from and free of all their biased considerations. Unless they be the satans in human form or animals in human dress, who imagine irreligion and atheism to be politics and support them.

"All praise be to God, because I withdrew from politics, I did not reduce the diamond-like truths of the Qur'an to the value of fragments of glass amid accusations of political propaganda. Indeed, the diamonds increase their value in the view of every group in brilliant fashion."[165] That is, keeping away from politics prevents the truths of the Qur'an that are valuable like diamonds from being reduced to pieces of glass.

Nursi answers the question, *"Why have you withdrawn from politics and now have nothing to do with it?"* as follows: *"The Old Said of nine or ten years ago was involved in politics to a degree; indeed, thinking he would serve religion and learning by means of politics, he was wearied for nothing. He saw that it is a dangerous way, which is dubious and full of difficulties, and for me superfluous as well as forming an obstacle to the most necessary duties. It is mostly lies and may be exploited by foreigners without one being aware of it.*

"Furthermore, a person who enters politics either wins or is in opposition. As for winning, since I am neither an official nor a deputy, to work

---

[165] Nursi, B. S., *The Letters*, The Thirteenth Letter, p. 66 (translation by Ş. Vahide), accessed September 29, 2014, www.dur.ac.uk/resources/sgia/imeis/Lets1-13.pdf.

in politics is unnecessary and nonsense for me. Politics has no need for me that I should meddle in them for nothing. If I join the opposition, I would do so either with ideas or with force. If it was with ideas there is no need for me, for the questions are all clear and everyone knows them as I do. To wag one's chin for nothing is pointless. If I join the opposition intending to use force and to provoke an incident, I might commit thousands of sins to reach one doubtful goal. Numerous people would be struck by disaster on account of one."[166]

Nursi answers the question, *"Why does the New Said avoid politics with such vehemence?"* as follows: *"He avoids it so vehemently in order to serve belief and the Qur'an, which is of the greatest importance, the greatest necessity and is the most pure and most right, in order not to sacrifice unnecessarily and officiously for one or two doubtful years of worldly life the working for and gaining of more than millions of years of eternal life. For he says: I am getting old and I do not know how many more years I shall live, so the most important question for me must be to work for eternal life. The prime means of gaining eternal life and the key to everlasting happiness is belief, so one has to work for that."*[167]

Nursi imposes it as "a fundamental principle" for those who are busy with the service of Islamic belief not to interfere in politics or matters of administration, and explains his reasoning as follows: *"A fundamental principle of the Risale-i Nur students is that as far as is possible they do not interfere in politics, or matters of administration, or government activities, because for them, working seriously for the Qur'an is worth everything, and is sufficient. Also, no one who enters politics, among the overwhelming currents that now prevail, can preserve his independence and sincerity. He is bound to become subject to one of the currents, and it will exploit him for worldly ends. It will corrupt the sacredness of his duty. Also, in the material struggle, due to the utter tyranny and despotism that is the rule this century, he would have to crush numerous innocent supporters of a person because of the error that person had made.*

---

[166] Nursi, B. S., *The Letters*, The Sixteenth Letter, p. 80-81 (translation by Ş. Vahide), accessed September 29, 2014, www.dur.ac.uk/resources/sgia/imeis/Lets15-18.pdf.

[167] Ibid., p. 81.

He would otherwise be defeated. It would also seem in the view of those who had given up their religion for the world, or who exploited it, that the Qur'an's sacred truths, which can be the tool of nothing, were being exploited for political propaganda. Also, every class of people, supporters and opposers, officials and common people, should have a share of those truths and all are in need of them. The Risale-i Nur students have therefore to avoid politics and the material struggle completely, and not be in any way involved in them, so that they may remain completely impartial."[168]

He gives himself as an example about keeping away from politics: "*All of my friends who contact me know that let alone interfering in politics, it is contrary to my real aim, mood, and holy service of Islamic belief to try to go into and even to think about politics. I was given the light, not the club of politics. One wisdom behind this state is as follows: I think God Almighty put a coldness and hatred toward politics in my heart so as not to deprive the people who are interested very much in the truths of belief and who are government officials of the truths of belief and in order to prevent them from having a worried and critical attitude toward them.*"[169]

Nursi states that religion should not be used negatively, that is, in a way that will cause negative perceptions and reactions in the country. He says such attitudes mean strengthening the hands of the enemies of Islam; he asks people to avoid, in principle, deeds that will make the enemies of Islam happy: "*Yes, the religion is served by making people be inclined to the religion, encouraging them to cling to the religion and reminding them about their religious duties. If one addresses them as 'You are irreligious,' it causes them to attack Islam. The religion cannot be used in a negative (destructive) way in the country. A person who was a caliph for thirty years used Islam in politics; you saw the harm inflicted on sharia because of it. Do you know who will make use of the fatwas of today's negative politicians? I think it is the most ferocious adversary of Islam; it stabbed its dagger in the lungs of Islam.*"[170]

---

[168] Nursi, B. S., *The Rays*, The Fourteenth Ray, p. 384 (translation by Ş. Vahide), accessed September 29, 2014, www.dur.ac.uk/resources/sgia/imeis/14Ray07.pdf.

[169] *Tarihçe-i Hayat*, p. 215.

[170] *Sünûhât*, p. 47.

Nursi stresses that the value of the truths of belief is above everything else in the universe, and to mix them with politics is to reduce their value. However, he points out that politicians should take the necessary steps to make it easier to carry out this religious service, since it contributes to social peace and public order: *"Service to faith and truths of belief are above everything else in this universe. They cannot be subject to or instrument to anything! However, at this time, in the eyes of the miserable and the wretched and the heedless people who sell religion for the world and exchange everlasting diamonds for pieces of glass, service to the Wise Qur'an absolutely prohibits us from involvement in politics out of concerns for making service to belief subject to or instrument to the strong external political currents and for lowering the high values of its truths in the eyes of all people. O people of politics and government! Do not busy yourselves with us out of unfounded fears. To the contrary, you should grant us an easy time. Because our service to religion helps to maintain peace and public order as well as saving social life from anarchy, and firmly lays, supports, and strengthens the cornerstones of your main task by establishing security, respect, and compassion."*[171]

In a true dream before the First World War, Nursi saw that Mount Ararat exploded into mountain-sized pieces scattered all over the world, and in this state of horror, he heard the command, *"Proclaim the miraculousness of the Qur'an!"* Nursi interpreted this dream as follows: *"I awoke and I understood that there was going to be a great explosion and upheaval, and that following it the walls surrounding the Qur'an would be destroyed. The Qur'an would then defend itself directly. It was going to be attacked and its miraculousness would be its steel armor. And in a way surpassing his ability, someone like myself would be appointed at this time to reveal one sort of its miraculousness; I understood that I had been designated."*[172] That is, there would be major social and political changes; the Ottoman Empire that protected the Qur'an for centuries from all kinds of attack like a great wall would collapse; state protec-

---

[171] *Tarihçe-i Hayat*, pp. 293–294.

[172] Nursi, B. S., *The Letters*, The Twenty-Eighth Letter, p. 424 (translation by Ş. Vahide), accessed September 29, 2014, www.dur.ac.uk/resources/sgia/imeis/Lets28-29_1_.pdf.

tion would end; and Qur'an would defend itself with the power of its truths without needing the guardianship of any political or military power. The miraculousness of the Qur'an would protect itself from all attacks like a steel armor.

Nursi's work *Risale-i Nur*, which is an explanation and proof of the truths of the Qur'an, repelled all assaults to the Qur'an from all directions, and time has confirmed this dream and its interpretation. In the light of the reality of this dream and the service method of Nursi, it can be asserted that the time to safeguard religion by the state is over; and that from now on, the struggle between belief and disbelief will continue among individuals on the platform of freedom and in the arena of reason and intellect. This struggle will be won by those who conquer the minds and the hearts through information and communication, and not those who resort to the use of force and oppression by relying on the power of government.

In the past, when religion and the thought of the hereafter were dominant over the community, politics assumed a religious path somehow and became "Islamic politics" in the Islamic world. At the times when the religion was in the center of the individual and social life, it was a natural sociological phenomenon for religion to play a central role in politics and shape politics. Politics, which enters the service of religion, strengthened and spread religion both in the Islamic and Christian world. However, in recent times, when the attractiveness of the worldly life settled in the center of the individual and social life predominantly, a breakdown occurred and religion was pushed aside from the center. And politics replaced religion with intellect, science and freedom, which are the rising values of this century, and aimed to give its members the best material interests of the world. The difference of opinion in reaching that aim brought about various political movements; and the political grounds became the area of conflict for the interest groups under the arbitration of modern values.

While many prominent religious figures advocated to earn religion a central spot through politics, as in the past, and to make it the dominant force even by resorting to force if necessary by using the resources of the state, Nursi adopted just the opposite approach. To him, the time for imposing religion on others by taking over the government via politics is over, and wishing this is wishing the impossible in this modern age when humanity has awakened, imitation and trust have shattered, the attractive worldly life has become the aim, individual rights and freedoms such as the freedoms of conscience and expression have risen, religious and state affairs have separated, governorship has been reduced from being a master to being a servant as the public is elevated from being a servant to being a master, and reason, science, and public opinion rule. Such an approach would result in the perception that religion is a political instrument, and it will set the ground for attacks to religion. This will cause people who are in opposing movements to oppose religion even more and deviate from it. Therefore, if religion and politics are mixed in this age, politics would take the front seat while religion is confined to the back seat. Politicization of religion is not a service, but actually a disservice to religion, which is not supposed to be used as an instrument—just like the politicization of judicial system, military, and sciences bring harm, not good, and paralyzes them.

For this reason, Nursi stayed away from 'political Islam,' and instead took 'civil Islam' (or 'personal Islam') as a base. He aimed to win the minds and the hearts of individuals through rational thinking and reasoning, and not high government posts via politics, and to turn attentions from the worldly matters to afterlife concerns. He chose as his goal to save the beliefs of people and to secure eternal happiness rather than helping people gain temporary worldly benefit.

One's intentions need to be pure, sincere, and free from ulterior motives for his message to echo in the minds and the hearts. This is only possible by remaining distant from all sorts of worldly benefits, and thus from politics, and this is exactly what Nursi did by running away from politics as he would from Satan. He exemplified with his life that the most effective service to religion in this age of freedoms can be done by staying away from politics. This is the secret behind Nursi's success in engraving the truths of the Qur'an on millions of mind and hearts through *Risale-i Nur*. And Nursi has done this by recognizing and working within the framework of the values and realities of the time, and not by colliding with them. The governments at the time tried with all their might and resources to discredit and stop Nursi's struggle which he started in exile as a lonely and powerless man away from politics, but it failed. That is, in a struggle between an individual and a state for winning the minds and the hearts of people, a weak individual has defeated a strong state. This should serve as a lesson for those who think that religion can be served effectively only by being strong and through politics, and thus by acquiring high political posts and power.

The numerous experiences in the last century showed that religion and politics, jurisdiction and politics, military and politics, and science and politics are fatal mixtures; it is necessary to avoid these mixtures. Otherwise, these institutions will fall into a debatable state and lose their prestige in the eyes of the people; thus, they will be harmed and be unable to fulfill their functions. To involve these institutions, which need to remain pure and clean in their highest position in the eyes of the people, in politics with some short-run plans means to make them victims of politics and scapegoats. This is a big murder committed against these institutions, which need to unite people. Politicized religion, politicized jurisdiction, politicized military, and politicized science are very harmful for both the country and the people living in the country. The harms inflicted on Islam by the movements of the mixture of religion and politics and the negative image brought about by them are obvious. Keeping religion outside politics, Nursi preserved the respect and prestige of the institution of religion and prevented religion from being a simple political thing to be shoved, and from being attacked and opposed. It is necessary to try to keep religion outside politics in order to make it remain in the lofty position that it deserves and address the whole humanity.

Nursi is a true realist, and not an illusionist. He has read the dominant realities and values of the time correctly, and unveiled the face of Islam that is in concord with these values. Contrary to many, rather than taking people to another time and space to observe their religion or leaving them in a dilemma to lead double lives, he opened a window of Islam facing our time, and showed that Islam can perfectly be observed in harmony with the modern values of the time. Unlike many of his contemporaries, he viewed the modern platform of intellect, sciences, and technology as a firm ground for the religion rather than a threat, and filled his sails with the winds of the values of his time while others were thrown off course by the same winds. His expression *"in the future when reason, sciences, and technology rule, surely Qur'an, which relies on rational proofs and invites reason to confirm its pronouncements, will gain ascendancy,"*[173] is a statement that unites and to some degree equates religion and the intellect, and proclaims the good news that in the future there will be a mutual understanding and common peace and tranquility in the world instead of conflict. In this age of freedom and liberty, those who observe individual rights and freedoms, take virtue that includes all high moral values and ethics as the base, and embrace the dominant values of time such as justice, sciences, mutual consultation, and public opinion, will ascend, while those who are unaware of the change and rely on power and resort to oppression and despotism will decline.

---

[173] *Hutbe-i Şâmiye*, p. 26.

Chapter 7

Peace and Tranquility

There is tendency in humanity and the universe towards advancement and perfection. In the words of Nursi, *"In this tree of universe, there is tendency towards perfection. That is to say, all particles and components of the whole universe tend to perfection like a tree, and advances towards it. Apart from this tendency of perfection; there is tendency in mankind as well for advancement."*[174] As an outcome of this tendency, the universe and humanity are in constant change, and this change continues at an accelerated pace. There is an intense level of activity for better tomorrows, and everyone is in a race. The engine behind this change is the technology that is advancing at a head-spinning pace.

The capability of television screens and computer monitors to mirror an event as it is happening at millions of places at once whets the appetite of evil-minded people as well. An event that attracts the attention of printed and visual media is multiplied by these screens, and ends up having the impact of a million events. This magnified effect destroys the peace of mind of many, shatters hopes, and stabs spirits. An impact of this magnitude serves as a base for new ill-intentioned acts. For this reason, news media organizations have great duties and responsibilities in the fight against terror. A news organization that projects a terrorist act in graphic detail into all parts of the world and injects all destructive ingredients into millions of unsuspecting minds in the name of "fast and true journalism" is in fact the biggest partner of terrorists,

---

[174] *İşârâtü'l-İ'câz*, p. 119.

and lays the ground for new such acts. The principles, *"Everything you say must be right, but telling all the right things is not right,"*[175] and *"Description of falsehood in great detail misleads simple minds,"*[176] should be guides for news reporters.

Turning on the TV and watching the frightful events in the world with curiosity poses a serious threat to psychological and mental health, and leaves sensitive people in sorrow. Bediüzzaman cautions against knowingly harming oneself this way: *"Now everyone on the planet is disturbed either physically, or mentally, or psychologically, or emotionally from dreadful events, and is in pain and misery. In particular, the misguided and heedless suffer from the excruciating and horrendous pain of humanity because of their concern for others in addition to their own pain, since they are unaware of the general heavenly grace and encompassing and mysterious heavenly wisdom. Because they needlessly neglect their main duties and important obligations, and turn their attention with curiosity to external political fights and universal events and get mentally involved, their souls are shaken and their mind confused. . . . I am of the opinion that in these storms and fires of the globe, the ones that preserve the peace of the mind and the tranquility of the heart are those who truly believe and completely trust in God and be totally pleased with Him."*[177]

The real reason behind the concern for the clash of civilizations is not the conflicts or oppositions among civilizations; rather, it is the fear and distrust among the members of different civilizations. That is, it is the conceived phobia that stems from not knowing each other. Establishing an atmosphere of trust by forming closer and warmer relationships will dissipate these fears and will help establish global peace. Bediüzzaman explains the aggression of some minorities in the early part of the twentieth century in a similar manner: *"I think their aggression is in retaliation to the presumed aggression from you and a show of force against the conceived aggression from you. If they are totally convinced that there will be no aggression from you, they will be content*

---

[175] *Mektubat,* p. 300.
[176] Ibid., p. 530.
[177] *Kastamonu Lahikası,* p. 94.

with justice."[178] Presumed fears can be cause for war even today, and mutual trust can be established by eliminating such fears.

The historical fact that members of different religions have lived in Jerusalem and Palestine side by side for hundreds of years in peace and mutual trust during Ottoman times shows that global peace is possible so long as justice and basic human rights are observed and equality before law is upheld. If those people who come from a tradition of peace and respect are resorting to terror today, the causes behind it should be investigated. When those causes are eliminated, peace and tranquility will certainly return to that heartland.

One of the most basic and most important senses in people is the "sense of fear." This sense, which is given to preserve life, can ruin one's life instead and turn life into hell when abused. The ill-intentioned propagandists utilize this sense of fear a lot to shape public opinions. They can justify many atrocities and injustices by stirring this sense and blowing it out of proportion, and they can desensitize the public on matters that the public is normally sensitive about. The ill-intentioned people use the sense of fear as an effective weapon to engineer the reactions of a society.

Bediüzzaman stresses that living in constant fear destroys one's quality of life, and advises that even in personal matters it is better to overlook past animosities and establish peace: *"It occurred to me to explain a truth to you which will save you from both worldly torment and the torment of the hereafter. It is as follows: For example, a person killed someone's brother or one of his relatives. A murder which yields one minute's pleasure of revenge causes millions of minutes of both distress for the heart and the anguish of prison. And the fear of revenge by the murdered man's relatives, and anxiety of finding himself face to face with his enemy drives away all his pleasure in life. He suffers the torment of both fear and anger. There is only one solution for this, and that is reconciliation, which the Qur'an commands, and truth, reality, benefit, humanity, and Islam require and encourage. Certainly, what is required in reality is peace."*[179]

---

[178] *Münâzarât*, p. 31.
[179] Nursi, B. S., *The Words*, The Thirdteenth Word, p. 165 (translation by Ş. Vahide), accessed September 29, 2014, www.dur.ac.uk/resources/sgia/imeis/words11-14_07_.pdf.

Bediüzzaman states that nurturing animosity in the heart is animosity towards self, and he advises that those who love themselves should not allow the feeling of hostility and vengeance enter their hearts. This advice is equally valid for states. Well-aware of this, France and Germany buried their past animosity in history shortly after the World War II and poured the foundation of lasting peace—a movement that formed the foundation of the European Union, which is a growing union of lasting peace. With this act that prefers the mind to feelings, they virtually confirm Bismarck's following statement: "A real politician is not a person that takes the revenge of the previous incidents; he is the one that prevents them from occurring again."

The biggest obstacle in the path of the advancement of humankind, and thus general peace and tranquility, is bigotry that narrows people's angle of view, and causes them to view everything with suspicion and enmity. The reason for bigotry is ignorance, and its remedy is enlightenment with knowledge. Bediüzzaman states that the obstacle of bigotry has largely been disappeared with the advance of civilization: "*A person who puts on black glasses sees everything black and ugly. As such, if the perceptive eye of the person is veiled by hypocrisy, and his heart is wrapped with non-belief, everything will seem ugly and bad, and this may cause enmity and resentment towards all people and even the universe.*"[180]

In order to take sail forward and catch up with the times, it is necessary to read the flow of time well and to act accordingly. Otherwise, in football terms, one may find himself offside, and all efforts can go to waste. As it is unthinkable today to treat illnesses using the medical sciences and medicines of the last century, so it is impossible to solve the current problems of society and the world using the methods of the past. Today's problems are very different in scope and size from those of yesterday, and their solutions require very different approaches. For example, the actions of individuals and societies in the past were ruled by emotions rather than the mind and knowledge, and as a result, bigotry and disunity were commonplace. Individuals and societies were led by appealing to these emotions rather than convincing the mind with

---

[180] *İşârâtü'l-İ'câz*, p. 95.

reason. Nowadays the mind, sciences, justice, goodwill, and public interest rule instead of emotion; and the states that have adhered to these present-day values are rightfully called contemporary states. The backwardness of the states that have stuck to the past with bigotry and turned their back to contemporary values is worth thinking about. The states that have remained in the dark corners of the past should analyze this picture carefully.

The path of time and the route of the world show that humanity will adhere to contemporary values, and will unite around them. Bediüzzaman expresses this as follows: *"The school of emotions that is called the past and the academy of thoughts that is called the future are not of the same form."*

Firstly: *"What I mean by the people of the past are the people living before the sixteenth century in the middle and first ages except Muslims. In fact, Muslims were distinguished and superior for about three hundred years and were usually perfect for about five hundred years. I describe the period between the eleventh century and the eighteenth century as the past and the centuries after that as future.*

"It is known that the dominant thought in man after that period is either the mind or the eye; in other words, thoughts and feelings, the truth or power, wisdom or government, the inclinations of the heart or the mind, desires or guidance.

"Therefore, we see that the relatively simple manners and the pure emotions of the people of the past suppressed and ruled over their unenlightened minds, which resulted in the spread of individuality and division. However, the relatively enlightened minds of the people of the future took control over their blind emotions tainted with lust and desire and forced them to abide by the mind, which is assurance that justice for all is to become commonplace. Humanity has prevailed to some degree. It gives glad tidings that Islam, which is the real humanity, will shed light over the gardens of Asia like clear sun in the cloudless skies of the future."[181] The Islamic world should listen to this good news, and should strip itself from the baseless fears and hesitations and jump into the wagon

---

[181] *Muhâkemât*, pp. 24–25.

of our time. Those already in that wagon are not strangers—they are fellow human beings.

Those who look at wars, terrorist acts, hostilities, and tears in various parts of the world see no light of hope, and predict with pessimism that the differences will grow wider, and darker days are awaiting us in the future. Nursi, on the other hand, sees a totally different view when he looks at the future with the binoculars of faith and Divine wisdom: *"As has been established by the prying investigations and innumerable experiments of the sciences, the fundamental and absolutely overriding aim and the true purpose of the All-Glorious Maker in the order of the universe are good, beauty, excellence, and perfection. For all the physical sciences demonstrate such an order and perfection in the fields they study in accordance with their comprehensive laws that the intellect can find nothing more perfect."*[182] In the future, with the complete development of sciences and humanity, the human race will surely comply with this perfection in the universe, and prove that humanity is the greatest fruit of the tree of creation. *"As civilization, virtue, and freedom become more and more dominant in the world of humanity, the other side of the balance will necessarily get lighter and lighter."*[183]

---

[182] *Hutbe-i Şâmiye*, p. 38.
[183] *Münâzarât*, p. 29.

Chapter 8

Terror and Weapons of Mass Destruction

H uman beings are naturally inclined towards beauty, perfection, goodwill, and justice. They like these attributes and dislike their opposites that are ugliness, imperfection, selfishness, and injustice. A civilization can be a real civilization and become a means of progress only if it possesses high attributes. A criterion for this is to attract rather than repel, and to result in virtuous acts that human consciences can easily accept. Otherwise, it is a deceptive or even savage civilization, and it can lead humanity to disaster rather than happiness. A proof of this is that the technological advancements and the rapid industrialization in the first half of the twentieth century resulted in two world wars, the death of millions of people, and the near-ruin of the world. A system that benefits a small minority while leaving the great majority in poverty and deprivation cannot be a civilization.

The fruits of the current Western Civilization are not appealing at all. It appears that a small minority lives in wealth and luxury while most people live in poverty and even in hunger. This situation feeds the feelings of jealousy, hatred, animosity, and revenge, and if they are not controlled, these growing feelings can take over. A person under the control of these feelings can turn to acts such as theft, sabotage, murder, rebellion, and terror, and can ruin peace and tranquility in a society. Therefore, the current shortsighted Western Civilization that is based on 'self-interest' and 'self-gratification' is serving as a mechanism that destroys the peace in societies and even in the world. So it must budget a large amount of resources to eliminate these threats by police and military force.

Terror can be considered in two parts, and both are associated with the feelings of caring and compassion. The feelings of caring and compassion in people are the source of the tendencies of protecting the loved ones, eliminating the threats and dangers, and even attacking those who show hostility. Even fearful creatures—such as hens—are often observed turning into brave warriors when the feeling of compassion is stirred. If a strong belief and its outcomes, which are trust in God and submission to Him, do not completely rule in the heart, a person can lose control of himself as the feelings of compassion and care burst out under strong emotional distress such as the harassment or murder of loved ones, and the awakened feelings of revenge and destruction can control this normally peaceful person. The mind and the conscience can no longer keep the person from such acts, and the person becomes "temporarily insane." People whose intellectual faculties are disabled under such heavy emotional stress may not even be responsible for their acts, and in some legal systems, suffering from temporary insanity is a valid basis for the claim of innocence. Those who go after terror by using cruelty and force to deter others by instilling fear often spread the terror and cruelty by turning emotional people whose senses of compassion are injured into wounded lions—just like turning harmless bees into killer bees by inserting a stick into beehives. Such people may regret what they have done when things calm down and they come to their senses.

The reasons behind the more violent second kind of terror and anarchy are the corruption of the heart, the diminishing feelings of compassion and care due to the destruction of moral values, and the turning of people into wild beasts who are not disturbed by inflicting pain to others (or who even like it), like snakes. Such people have surfaced in recent years in growing numbers, and they are the real threat to the future of the civilization and humanity: As Nursi puts it, "*Socialism sprang up in the French Revolution from the seed of libertarianism. Then since socialism destroyed certain sacred matters, the ideas it inculcated turned into bolshevism. And because bolshevism corrupted even more sacred moral and human values, and those of the human heart, of course the seeds it sowed will produce anarchy, which recognizes no restrictions whatsoever and has respect for nothing. For if respect and compassion quit the human heart, those with such hearts become exceedingly cruel beasts and can no longer be governed through politics."*[184]

Fight against Terrorism

The biggest mistake in the fight against terror is to think that terror can be prevented by military and security measures since the terrorists are few by number and weak by resources. Superiority is not a valid criterion in the fight against terror because terror is destruction, and destruction is easy. Major damage can be done with little force. Sometimes a single person with a single match can burn a large area with many houses in it, and hundreds of firemen with their modern equipment may feel powerless fighting the fire. As Nursi puts it, *"For the most part, misguidance and evil are negative, destructive, and pertain to non-existence. While in the great majority of cases, guidance and good are positive, constructive, repairing, and pertain to existence. Everyone knows that one man can destroy in one day a building made by twenty men in twenty days. Yes, although human life continues through the existence of all the basic members and conditions of life, and is particular to the All-Glorious Creator's power, through severing a member, a tyrant may make the person manifest death, which is non-being in relation to life. The saying 'Destruction is easy' has for this reason become proverbial."*[185]

Any results obtained by offering rewards or instilling fear are temporary and superficial. An effective and lasting fight against terror is only possible by eliminating the causes that awaken, feed, and stir the senses of destruction and hostility in people. So long as these tendencies are alive and well, all efforts in fighting terror are bound to go to waste.

---

[184] Nursi, B. S., *The Rays*, The Fifth Ray, p. 109 (translation by Ş. Vahide), accessed September 29, 2014, www.dur.ac.uk/resources/sgia/imeis/2-6Rays_07_.pdf.

[185] Nursi, B. S., *The Flashes*, The Thirteenth Flash, pp. 104-105 (translation by Ş. Vahide), accessed September 29, 2014, www.dur.ac.uk/resources/sgia/imeis/2Fl0981-156.pdf.

This can be achieved by subscribing to truth and fairness that rule over minds, warm the hearts, and establish control over human conscience. Nursi expresses this concisely as follows: "*With the deception of motivation and intimidation one can only have a superficial effect and keep the mind in line. Impinging into the depths of the heart, moving even the most delicate senses, flourishing the inner talents like a blossoming rose, shaking and mobilizing the hidden and dormant talents and tendencies, causing the essence of humanity to gush out, and exhibiting the value of articulation are from the glimpses of the rays of truth. Yes, polishing of the hearts from revolting practices such as burying of girls while alive, which is a monument of stone heartedness, and gilding the hearts with virtues like mercy to animals, even compassion to ants, which is a flash of delicacy and tenderness, are such great revolutions— especially in such ignorant and stubborn tribes—that, because no natural laws are utilized, all observant and truthful people will admit that this is extraordinary.*"[186]

The most effective and civilized way of fighting flies is via cleanliness. This is because flies multiply in dirty places, and smelly dirt attracts them. Fighting flies with chemicals is both expensive and short-lived, and it poses risks to those exposed to the chemicals. Besides, the garbage dumps will continue to serve as production sites of flies so long as they exist, and the only winners from this fight will be the chemical companies. Also, mosquitoes can be fought most effectively by getting rid of swamps or by treating them properly when the mosquitoes are still larvae. Likewise, the most effective treatment against pests like anarchy, murder, transgression, and terror that threaten today's civilization is to dry up the swamps of selfishness, exploitation, and injustice that produce and feed them by the medicines of compassion, assistance, and justice. That is, to treat today's civilization with heavenly principles that prescribe compassion and justice as a basis in all affairs. Otherwise, resorting to force instead of compassion and strength instead of justice cannot get rid of these pests; to the contrary, the use of force causes those pests to spread and multiply faster, exposing the world to a greater danger.

---

[186] *Muhâkemât*, p. 111.

We call up on those whose hearts are hard towards the needy but budget billions of dollars to fight terror: You can solve this problem permanently and at much lower cost and by changing hostilities to friendships. The way to such a solution passes from being civilized not only in the body but also in the soul; that is, from virtue. Otherwise, all of your money and the effort will go to waste. Terror will be increasing rather than decreasing, and you will lose more sleep over it.

Intellect and Public Opinion

As Nursi often expresses, different things are fashionable in different times, and different trends rule. Those who are not aware of the valuable commodities of their time and do not see the way time is flowing are like those who row against the current, and their entire effort is bound to go to waste. In old times, the engine of the time machine was force. But in these modern times, it is the mind, compassion, and conscience that rule, and those who fail to see this will fall down no matter how strong they are. Their hammer will strike on their heads first. In the words of Nursi, "*The ruler of the old times was strength; the one with the sharp sword and a stony heart would rise. But the motor, the soul, the strength, the ruler, and the boss of the times of freedom are righteousness, mind, knowledge, law, and public opinion. Only those with a sharp mind and a bright heart will rise to the top. Since knowledge increases with aging and strength decreases with growing old, the Middle-age states that are based on strength are destined to collapse while the contemporary states being founded on knowledge will have a Khidr-like (eternal) life.*" "*Your bosses, chiefs, and even spiritual leaders, if founded on strength and maintain sharp swords, will necessarily fall, and this is what they deserve. Those who stand on reason, utilize love instead of force, and keep their mind over their emotions, will not fall; they may even rise further.*"[187] Nursi explains how the developed countries can be caught up with and even passed: "*You can beat them with the same weapons that they*

---

[187] *Münâzarât*, p. 33.

beat you: the mind, the idea of nationalism, fondness of progress, and sense of justice."[188]

Nursi warns those who fail to see the necessities of the time and the direction of the world, and insist on using brutal force rather than the mind, love, and conscience: *"As for the one who strikes with the sword, the sword turns back and hits his own innocent. Now victory is not with the sword. There is a place for the sword, but it is the hand of the mind."*[189] The events in recent years seem to confirm this assessment. Those who resorted to brutal force and even suicide bombers—even for a right cause—are labeled as terrorists, and bring misery and tears to their people rather than victory and happiness. Likewise, even the superpowers who thought they were so powerful that they could do anything but were unaware of the reality of time have hit the invisible wall of time, and shot themselves with their own weapons.

Judging from the realities of time that Nursi brought to our attention we can say: Those who invest in arms and brutal force as they had been doing in the past are investing in nothing. Those who invest in the mind, sciences, research, love, justice, and public opinion will see their investment multiply, and achieve all of their goals easily—even if they are weak in armed forces. Those who think they can achieve their just cause by resorting to brutal force and terror sparked by the feelings of revenge and hostility should put aside these negative feelings and reevaluate their approach with a clear mind—if, of course, they want to put an end to their humiliation and suffering. Also, those who spend their time and resources to develop or acquire nuclear or other weapons of mass destruction should wake up quickly from these dreams whose time has passed. Otherwise, these weapons will strike the invisible wall of time, and explode on their own heads.

Technical work conducted with no regard to the basic principles of sciences will definitely result in failure. Likewise, any action incompatible with social principles, the realities of the situation, and the realities of time is bound to backfire and end in failure. Those who ask for

---

[188] Ibid., p. 68.
[189] Ibid.

the help of God should first obey the laws and principles God has dictated in this universe. Otherwise, he will be viewed as a rebel, and his request will be rejected. As Nursi puts it, *"Whoever wants Divine help, should familiarize himself or herself with Divine laws, creation, and nature, and work in accordance. Otherwise, the nature will give an answer of 'no' by denying the request. The general flow of things, on the other hand, will throw those who go in the opposite direction to a hole of nonexistence."*[190]

Weapons of Mass Destruction

In a world which is getting smaller and smaller and is interwoven with a network of communication, it has become extremely difficult to go against the general opinion of the public, and the common conscience of the public has become the biggest obstacle in the use of the weapons of mass destruction. A proof of this is the fact that although many wars have been fought since World War II, no country has dared to use nuclear weapons, including the United States, which lost over 50,000 soldiers in the Vietnam War. The only thing that can possibly justify the use of nuclear weapons is the fear of being attacked by such weapons, and it can be said that the best assurance against being attacked by nuclear or other weapons of mass destruction is to close the door firmly to these kinds of weapons.

Nursi labels the verse *"No bearer of burdens can bear the burdens of another"* (al-An'am 6:164) as *"the fairest Qur'anic principle,"* and explains the verse *"One who kills a person who has not killed anyone or has not caused public unrest in the world is like one who has killed all people"* (al-Maeda 5:32) as *"a person's life or blood cannot be sacrificed even for the entire humanity. Both are equivalent from the point of view of power, as they are equivalent from the point of view of justice."*[191] In light of these explanations, it is unthinkable for a Muslim to use a weapon of mass destruction that may cause the annihilation of countless innocent men, women, children, animals, and trees. This rule is also confirmed by the supreme religious councils in Egypt and Iran. The excuse

---

[190] *Muhâkemât*, p. 112.
[191] *Sünûhât*, p. 11.

of trying to obtain these weapons with the purpose of deterrence, not with the purpose of using them, is not believable.

The destruction of all weapons of mass destruction—including nuclear weapons—in the possession of Islamic states, ending of any research and development programs on such weapons, and the declaration to the whole world that, even when they are bombarded with such weapons, they will never respond in kind because they view the use of such weapons as a inhumane behavior and savagery, will have the effect of an atomic bomb in the shattering of the thick walls of fear and prejudice built around Islam and Muslims and the exposure of the core of Islam filled with love and compassion. It should not be forgotten that even today the expressed reason for many wars is "preemptive strike against a probable attack." The elimination of baseless fears and suspicions will eliminate the justifications for such wars, and the world will become a safer place.

Nursi asserts that the claim that the tension and distrust between the Western World and the Islamic World is leading towards the clash of civilizations stems from baseless fears and misconceptions, and states that these clouds of baseless fears that block the rays of the Islam will be wiped out by education that equips people with the desire to seek the truth, the love of humanity, and the human conscience: *"The biggest barrier between us and the Westerners is the baseless fears of clashing and refutation stemming from deceptive imagination related the extremities of Islam and scientific matters. Bravo to the enlightening support of schools and the factual support of sciences for equipping the truth with the tendency to investigate, the love of humanity, and the human conscience and for shattering those barriers then and now. Yes, the biggest causes that deprived us from the comfort of this world and the Westerners from the happiness in the hereafter and curtailed the sun of Islam are the misunderstandings and the baseless fears of clashing and opposition."*[192]

Nursi often states that the *Risale-i Nur* collection, which unifies physical and social sciences with religious teaching, serves as a guard-

---

[192] *Muhâkemât*, p. 5.

ian of peace, and the moral damage in the minds and hearts of people can be repaired only by moral atomic bombs: *"Now in all mankind, treaties are signed and measures are taken to protect humanity from corruption and to preserve general peace. . . . Risale-i Nur's preserving of peace in this land and nation—although there are more causes to disturb peace and safety here compared to other nations—shows that the establishment of that Eastern University will help humanity to enjoy general peace. This is because the damage nowadays is moral, and thus there ought to be a curative moral atomic bomb to repair it. A definite proof for the damage in this time and age being moral and this damage can possibly be counteracted only by curative moral atomic bombs is the Risale-i Nur's standing as a barricade against the attacks of misguidance, materialistic philosophy, and atheism within this thirty years. Risale-i Nur has become a restorer and moral atomic bomb against this morality damage."*[193]

---

[193] *Emirdağ Lahikası-*2, pp. 170–171.

Chapter 9

Terror and Islam

L ike every bright object reflecting the sunlight, and every transparent object containing a little sun in it, the good or bad acts of individuals reflect upon the members of the community they belong to, and one act becomes a thousand and even a million acts, depending on the size of the community. As Nursi puts it, *"Through the bond of this sacred nationhood, all the people of Islam become like a single tribe. Like the members of a tribe, the peoples and groups of Islam are bound and connected to one another through Islamic brotherhood. ... If a member of one tribe commits a crime, all the members of the tribe are guilty in the eyes of another, enemy tribe. It is as though each member of the tribe had committed the crime so that the enemy tribe becomes the enemy of all of them. That single crime becomes like thousands of crimes. And if a member of the tribe performs a good act that is the cause of pride affecting the heart of the tribe, all its members take pride in it. It is as if each person in the tribe feels proud at having done that good deed. It is because of this fact that at this time, and particularly in forty to fifty years' time, evil and bad deeds will not remain with the perpetrator; they will transgress the rights of millions of Muslims. Numerous examples of this shall be seen in forty to fifty years' time."*[194] *"Now a sin does not remain as 'one,' it becomes 'one thousand.'"*[195]

The silence of the Islamic world towards terror stemming from Muslims and its lack of reaction is astonishing. It looks as if siding with

---

[194] *Hutbe-i Şâmiye*, p. 53.
[195] *Münâzarât*, p. 66.

fellow Muslims in disputes with others is a necessary part of religious brotherhood. But Islam is truthfulness, and a Muslim can support only truthful acts. *"Truthfulness is the basis and foundation of Islam, and the bond between people of good character, and the basis of elevated emotions. Since this is so, as the foundation of the life of our society, we must bring to life truthfulness and honesty, and cure our moral and spiritual sicknesses with them. Yes, truthfulness and honesty are the vital principles in the life of Islamic society."*[196]

Islam and terror are the opposites of each other, just like day and night; and a terrorist destroys Islam first. Supporting all acts of a Muslim is not religious zeal; it is simply blind partisanship. Supporting an unjust act in the name of Islam is injustice to Islam first. It causes Islam to be equated to injustice, and it builds a dark wall and blocks the beauty of Islam. In the words of Bediüzzaman, *"A person is not liked for who he is; but more likely for his attributes and workmanship. Therefore, every attribute of every Muslim does not necessarily have to be Muslim, and all attributes and works of every nonbeliever do not necessarily have to be nonbelievers."*[197]

In fact, true love and loyalty to Islam requires fighting against those who misrepresent Islam. The past verdicts about the roundness of the earth can shed light on this matter: *"Imam al-Ghazali passed this verdict: 'Whoever denies and refuses to believe an act such as the roundness of the earth whose validity is based on definite evidence on the grounds of religious zeal, commits a major crime against the religion. For, this is treason, not loyalty.' ... Husayn al-Jisri threatens the nonbeliever of the roundness of the earth with a loud voice, and declares with the strength of the truth with no hesitation that 'whoever denies the roundness of the earth on the basis of religion with religious zeal is a fool friend, who causes greater harm than a severe enemy.'"*[198]

As stated clearly, those who do wrong in the name of religion—no matter how loyal and good-willed they are—cause more harm to the religion than the fiercest enemy of the religion. *"An ignorant friend can*

---

[196] *Hutbe-i Şâmiye*, p. 45.
[197] *Münâzarât*, p. 32.
[198] *Muhâkemât*, p. 41.

cause as much harm as an enemy. Until now, I used to watch the enemy only and break their transgression with the diamond sword at hand. But now I am obliged to bring those friends in line, I will use that sword to poke into their uneducated and excessive dreams."[199] For this reason, fighting those who do wrong in the name of religion is like fighting the enemies of religion. From the destruction-natured souls armed with hostility, we can expect only destruction and hostility—even if they are watered with Islam. *"The bee drinks water and makes honey; the snake drinks water and makes poison."*[200] Likewise, the delicate sunlight that enlightens the world can cause the things with a tendency to go bad to decompose and stink.

For Muslims, to support and to side with each other in wrongdoing is not necessarily due to Islamic brotherhood; rather, it may be due to political partisanship. Nursi expressed the criterion for it as follows: "*Whoever prefers his impious political partner to his pious opponent ill-intentioned excuses, he is motivated by politics. One who claims with possessiveness that his party is better suited to represent the religion, the sacred item that belongs to all, and in so doing stirs emotions against the religion and damages the image of religion in minds of great majority, is motivated by partisanship.*"[201]

Nursi often states that the time for armed struggle has passed, and that the struggle from now on will be by good acts and progress in all areas: "*In the past, Islam's progress occurred through smashing the enemy's bigotry and obstinacy and through defense against their aggression; through weapons and the sword. Whereas in the future, in place of weapons, the immaterial, moral swords of true civilization, material progress, and truth and justice will defeat and scatter the enemies.*"[202]

Humanity is transposing from the age of savagery and ignorance to the age of civilization and knowledge. In a world that has completed the phase of civilization, any wars can only be with words rather than arms. Those who conquer the minds with reason and elegance will con-

---

[199] Ibid., p. 37.
[200] *Münâzarât*, p. 80.
[201] *Sünûhât*, p. 48.
[202] *Hutbe-i Şâmiye*, p. 35.

quer the world. *"The way of this Union is love; its enmity is only for igno-rance, poverty, and strife. Non-Muslims should feel sure that this Union attacks only those three facts. Our actions towards non-Muslims consist only of persuasion, for we know them to be civilized. And we suppose them to be fair-minded, so we should demonstrate that Islam is lovable and elevated."*[203]

Nursi expresses that the time for hostilities has passed, and now is time for love: *"What I am certain of from my experience of social life and have learnt from my lifetime of study is the following: The thing most worthy of love is love, and that most deserving of enmity is enmity. That is, love and loving, which render man's social life secure and lead to hap-piness are most worthy of love and being loved. Enmity and hostility are ugly and damaging, have overturned man's social life, and more than anything deserve loathing and enmity and to be shunned. The time for enmity and hostility has finished. Two world wars have shown how evil, destructive, and what an awesome wrong is enmity. It has become man-ifest that enmity contains no good."*[204]

Terror associated with Islam has been in the world agenda for years, but the Islamic world's sidestepping the issue and failure to take a clear position on terror have strengthened preconceptions that tie Islam with terror. The weakness of individual reactions to terror and their inconsistency has neither had any significant effect on Muslims nor has it been sufficient to correct the tainted image of Islam. This both-ers the sincere Muslims who feel every stabbing to Islam in their chests, and leads them into hopelessness and dismay. The main reason behind this insensitivity, despair, and the anarchy of ideas is the absence of an authority, and this deficiency should be remedied right away. This vacant position should be filled not by one person, as in the past, but by a committee that is composed of twenty to thirty distinguished schol-ars of the Islamic world. The Muslims of the world will trust such an authority that forms a representative body, will follow its authorita-tive rulings, and will ignore the weak individual voices opposing the verdicts of such authority. This mechanism will also expose the evil-

---

[203] Ibid., p. 90.
[204] Ibid., p. 51.

doers who currently find the area wide open to spoil the unsuspecting innocent minds, and ensure that those evildoers are not welcome. *"A single piece of truth is superior to a lot of dreams."*[205] This way, the unfounded fears that leave Islam and Muslims under suspicion will disappear, despair will be replaced by hope, and the assessment *"The key and discloser of the continent of Asia and its future is mutual consultation"*[206] will be realized.

As stated previously, Nursi expresses the need for a high consulting committee as follows: *"This committee should be formed such that the Islamic world can trust this position. It should serve both as a source and as a position of reflection of ideas. It should be able to carry out its religious duties towards the Islamic world completely. We no longer live in old times. In the past, the governing authority was a single person. The advisor of that person on religious affairs could also be a single individual. He could verify or modify the ruler's ideas. But the time now is the time for collaboration and community. The governing body is a collective personality extracted out of the spirit of the community who is rather insensitive, kind of deaf, and strong, and the consulting bodies represent that spirit. A governing body of this sort should have an in-kind religious advisor, which should be a collective personality that borne out of a consulting body of prominent scholars. This way, it can make its voice heard, and can lead people to the right path from points related to religion. Otherwise, even if the individual is a genius, a single person will sound like a mosquito compared to the collective personality of the community."*[207]

Terror and Belief

True faith, which is a source of love, and terror, which is an outbreak of hatred and hostility, cannot be associated. It is unfortunate that the dominance of the feeling of hostility on a person to the point of ultimate sacrifice of one's life is confused with the apex of belief that prohibits

---

[205] *Muhâkemât*, p. 17.
[206] *Hutbe-i Şâmiye*, p. 60.
[207] *Sünûhât*, p. 33.

people from knowingly stepping on ants. The deepest sleep is thought to be awakening; and as Nursi puts it: *"In my youth I used to think that I reached the highest point of awakening. Now I understand that that awakening was not really awakening; it was the state of being in the deepest well of sleep. . . . Their example is like a sleeping person who supposedly wakes up in his dream and tells his dream to others. Where in fact, the waking up in the dream is indication that he has left the light level of the sleep and entered into the deep and heavy level. Such a sleeper is like the dead."*[208] Those who resort to terror in the name of Islam should be shaken forcefully and awoken from this deep confusion.

A fundamental principle of Islam is to love for God, to dislike for God, and to judge for God. Otherwise, people act by the desires of their soul, and commit injustice instead of justice. Islam, which should be a darling to the hearts, is equated with fear and terror as a result. Nursi narrates the following exemplary story: *"Imam Ali, may God be pleased with him, once threw an unbeliever to the ground. As he drew his sword to kill him, the unbeliever spat in his face. He released him without killing him. The unbeliever said: 'Why did you not kill me?' He replied: 'I was going to kill you for the sake of God. But when you spat at me, I became angered, and the purity of my intention was clouded by the inclinations of my soul. It is for this reason that I did not kill you.' The unbeliever replied: 'If your religion is so pure and disinterested, it must be the truth.'"*[209]

Nursi strongly warns those who use religion for politics: *"A person controlled by not the holy principles of 'to love for God, to dislike for God' but, God forbid, by the devilish principles of 'to love for politics, to dislike for politics,' showing hostility towards an angel-like true brother and love towards an evil political friend and approving his cruelties, may morally become a partner in those cruelties as well."*[210]

Signs that it is the belief that rules in the heart rather than the soul and desires are: to turn his face to the hereafter rather than the world, to be concerned with the sides of events facing the hereafter rather than the world, and to value the world only because it is the prepara-

---

[208] *Mesnevî-i Nuriye*, p. 114.
[209] *Mektubat*, p. 304.
[210] *Kastamonu Lahikası*, p. 94.

tion ground of the hereafter. During the World War II when even some religious persons and scholars were leaving the congregation in the mosques and racing to listen to the radio, Nursi was asked why he did not show any interest in the war, which had plunged the world into chaos and was closely connected with the fate of the Islamic world, and he was also asked *"if there is some event more momentous than the war."* He responded by saying *"Yes, an event more momentous than this World War and a case more important than that of world supremacy . . . is that for everyone the case has opened by which they may either win, in return for belief, or lose, eternal properties as broad as the earth set with palaces and gardens. If they do not secure the document of belief, they will lose. And this age, many are losing the case because of the plague of materialism."*[211] Also, even during the Battle of Badr, which is the most critical battle in Islamic history, the soldiers performed their prayers in congregation by the order of the Prophet, and earning the reward of congregation is preferred over the greatest event in the world.[212] This being the case, can a true believer with a sound mind disregard the severe threat of the Qur'an: *"One who kills a person who has not killed anyone or has not caused public unrest in the world is like one who has killed all people,"* (al-Maeda 5:32) and risk his eternal life by resorting to terrorist acts? If he does, this shows a major weakness in belief, and this person must cure this most dangerous illness in his heart first.

Individuals can determine their level of belief by weighing the feelings of brotherhood and hostility in their hearts: *"Belief establishes real brotherhood, connection, unification, and solidarity among all things. But non-belief, like chill, exhibits all things as unrelated to one another, and portrays them as strangers to one another. For this reason, there is no enmity, hostility, and violence in the spirit of a believer. He has some level of brotherhood even with his greatest enemy."*[213]

Risale-i Nur students have always been preservers of peace, and have remained distant to all forms of terror and anarchy. This is because

---

[211] Nursi, B. S., *The Rays*, The Eleventh Ray, pp. 223–224 (translation by Ş. Vahide), accessed September 29, 2014, www.dur.ac.uk/resources/sgia/imeis/7-11Rays07.pdf.

[212] *Emirdağ Lahikası-2*, p. 229.

[213] *Mesnevî-i Nuriye*, pp. 60–61.

the core of the *Risale-i Nur* is compassion and the fortification of belief. Millions of *Risale-i Nur* students are witnesses that the most effective way of fighting terror is to acquire true belief. "*Compassion, truth and right, and conscience, the fundamental way of the Risale-i Nur, severely prohibit us from politics and from interfering in government. For dependent on one or two irreligious people fallen into absolute unbelief and deserving of slaps and calamities are seven or eight innocents—children, the sick and the elderly. If slaps and calamities are visited on the one or two, those unfortunates suffer also. . . . Five principles are necessary, essential, at this strange time in order to save the social life of this country and nation from anarchy: respect, compassion, refraining from what is prohibited (haram), security, the giving up of lawlessness and being obedient to authority. The evidence that when the Risale-i Nur looks to the life of society it establishes and strengthens these five principles in a powerful and sacred fashion and preserves the foundation-stone of public order, is that over the last twenty years the Risale-i Nur has made one hundred thousand people into harmless, beneficial members of this nation and country.*"[214]

A strong belief is a barrier against all injustice, including terror. When a believer is overcome by the feeling of revenge and is inclined to annihilate innocent lives, the verdict revealed from the Divine Throne comes to his mind. Through the sense of belief and ear of the heart, it seems as though he hears the verses, "*No bearer of burdens can bear the burdens of another*" (al-An'am 6:164) and "*One who kills a person who has not killed anyone or has not caused public unrest in the world is like one who has killed all people*" (al-Maeda 5:32). These Divine commands activate belief, which stir the intellect, heart, conscience, spirit, and other elevated inner emotions into action. The mobilization of these faculties gives rise to strong waves, and the intellect, heart, spirit, conscience, and the inner faculties attack the extinction tendency that comes from the soul and lust, and silence it. At the end, that tendency subsides, and the person decides not to commit the evil deed. Otherwise, the idea of getting caught and the fear of being imprisoned alone

---

[214] Nursi, B. S., *The Rays*, The Fourteenth Ray, p. 372 (translation by Ş. Vahide), accessed September 29, 2014, www.dur.ac.uk/resources/sgia/imeis/14Ray07.pdf.

may not the strong enough to stop that evil tendency. As Nursi puts it, *"Belief places in the heart and mind a permanent 'prohibitor'; when sinful desires emerge from the soul, it repulses them, declaring: 'it is forbidden!' Man's actions result from the inclinations of his heart and emotions. They come from the sensibilities of the spirit and its needs. The spirit is stirred into action through the light of belief. If an act is good, he does it; if it is evil, he tries to restrain himself. Blinder emotions will not drive him down the wrong road and defeat him."*[215]

To Punish Other People due to the Mistake of Somebody Else

Unlike animals, no limit is put on the ability of people by their nature to do good or evil. The unbounded tendencies and feelings such as rebelling, injustice, and fearlessness, if left uncontrolled, can lead into great destruction. *"With selfishness, one can turn into such a person that he wishes to destroy everything that stands on the path of his desires and yearning, even the whole world if he has the capability."*[216] The biggest injustice people commit is to punish many innocent people because of one's fault. Islam refuses this injustice with the most just principle, *"No bearer of burdens can bear the burdens of another"* (al-An'am 6:164).

Nursi explains the verse, *"Indeed, mankind is very unjust, very ignorant"* (al-Ahzab 33:72) as follows: *"Here is the terrifying ability of injustice in the nature of man. It means this: Unlike animals, the senses and tendencies of people are not limited. The tendency to commit injustice and the love for self can go very far. Yes, if self-concern, self-adoration, conceitedness, and pride and stubbornness, which are the ugly sides of selfishness and ego, join that tendency, the person can invent such greatest major sins that the humanity could not find a name for it as yet. As it is evidence for the necessity of the hell, its punishment can only be the hell."*[217]

"As an individual, a person possesses many attributes. If one attribute among them attracts a hostile behavior, the Divine law in Qur'an

---

[215] *Hutbe-i Şâmiye*, p. 76.
[216] *Sünûhât*, p. 11
[217] Ibid., p. 23.

6:164 necessitates that hostility be limited to that attribute only, and feel pity for the person who is a collection of innocent attributes and refrain from any transgression against the person. But that cruel and ignorant person, with his cruel nature, assails the rights of all innocent attributes because of a single at faulty attribute, and even becomes hostile to the person, still discontented, he extends his hostility to his relatives, and even to his colleagues."[218]

Today, such atrocities are committed in the name of fighting terror that the human conscience bursts out and rebels, and the feelings of destruction and hostility of victimized people are sharpened. As Nursi puts it, *"This civilization gives way to most horrible cruelties like if there is a traitor in a village, destroying that village together with its innocent people, or if there is a rebel in a community, to annihilate that community together with all including children, or if a person who refuses to obey the unjust laws takes refuge in a sacred building like the Hagia Sophia which is worth billions, to destroy that building. If, from a fairness point of view, a man cannot be held responsible before God for the sins committed by his brother, how can it be that, thousands of uninvolved innocents of a town or community, in a place that is never free of bad-natured rebels or the uprising of a stubborn person, can be held responsible and even be annihilated."*[219]

Judging on the Basis of the Outcome

The primary reasons behind divisions and clashing of ideas in the Islamic World are the examination and evaluation of issues from a narrow perspective, the disregard of the effects of changing times and conditions, and the inadequate involvement of the mind and reason. However, *"Every time or age has its own verdicts. The time we are in decrees the prohibition and abolition of some aged traditions. Having more evil than good calls for a verdict of death for such traditions."*[220] The Qur'an also encourages people to think and to use their minds.

---

[218] Ibid., p. 24.
[219] Ibid., p. 25.
[220] *Münâzarât*, p. 63.

Nursi attracts attention to the probable results when evaluating events and ideas: *"Look at the evidence and the consequences.... What distinguish alike trees are their fruits. Therefore, look at the consequences of my ideas and their ideas. In one it is rest and compliance. Hidden in the other are unrest and loss."*[221] "The thing that shows the essence of something is its fruit."[222] Nursi warns those who fail to see the changing conditions of the world and dream about living in the past: *"I will tell you something very short. You can memorize it. Here it is: The old way is no way; either new way or way to grave."*[223]

Those who resort to terror in the name of Islam and view this as a virtue should examine the consequences of these acts very carefully, and think about who benefits from such acts and the kinds of cruelty such acts lay the groundwork for, and answer these questions: After these terrorist acts, is it the friendship of people to Islam that has increased or is it hostility? Has the name of Islam been elevated or tainted? Has the image and standing of Muslims in the world improved, or are Muslims now being perceived as horrifying savages whose hearts are filled with hatred and hostility and who get pleasure out of bloodshed and murder? Do people's hearts feel warmer towards Islam or colder? Have the injustice and cruelty that initiated the terror ended or decreased, or have they returned more heavily and caused more pain and suffering for many more innocent people?

It appears that the only thing terror has accomplished is to lay the groundwork and to serve as a justification for all these negatives and cruelties. It is hard to see the kind of logic and reasoning behind the insistence on wrongdoing and failing to recognize the magnitude of damage caused. Nursi points out that *"the origin of Islam is knowledge, and its foundation is the mind,"* and states that *"accepting the truth and rejecting the unfounded falsehood"* is the reputation of Islam.[224] He also brings to our attention that *"Islam calls on and encourages reason and knowledge and protects scholars"* as witnessed with verses from Qur'an

---

[221] Ibid., p. 15.

[222] Ibid., p. 17.

[223] Ibid.

[224] *İşârâtü'l-İ'câz*, p. 105.

such as *"So will they not think?" (Ya-Sin 36:68), "So will they not reason?" (al-An'am 6:50) and "So will they not ponder on it?" (an-Nisa 4:82).*[225] What needs to be done is to evaluate the events and the words in the light of the mind, knowledge, and conscience before accepting or rejecting them.

---

[225] Nursi, B. S., *The Letters*, The Twenty-Sixth Ray, p. 376 (translation by Ş. Vahide), accessed September 29, 2014, www.dur.ac.uk/resources/sgia/imeis/Lets24-26. pdf.

Chapter 10

The Reality of Globalization

G lobalization is thought to be a twentieth-century concept, but it can be said that its existence is as old as the existence of the globe. Those who reside on the globe are naturally global since they are members and components of the same globe. That is, being part of the world community is a common feature for all of them. Therefore, the real intent behind 'globalization' is the extent and nature of it, and the degree it affects individuals and societies.

The region of interest of early men was naturally bound by the distance they could walk or ride on their animals, and their primary occupation was to provide for their daily needs. Therefore, living as tribes was well-suited for the simple lifestyle of those times, and each tribe was like a globe of its own. The advancement of humankind and the increase in common needs resulted in collaborations at higher levels, and the formation of nations and states. Today, the advances made in the transportation and communication technologies, the rapid rise in the standard of living, and being more civilized and socially oriented has brought about extensive collaborations among nations and even continents, and thus globalization is at the level of the globe, which is the last stage of globalization.

Recent developments in communication technologies have put a globe in the living room of each house, and an event in a distant corner of the world can affect the lives of everyone everywhere. We are saddened by the sorrow of the people we see on the TV screen, and rejoice in their happiness. An event of general interest, such as the Olympics, can turn all people into a family and the whole world into a living room.

The use of the Internet in recent years at an increasing rate has amplified the flow of information and accelerated globalization. Now, everybody is becoming a 'world citizen' in a real sense, and being from a country in the world does not mean much more than being from a city in a country. People are being judged on the basis of their knowledge and ability, rather than their nationality.

Nursi expresses this phase and the reality that the world is becoming like a village as follows: "*Before the time of the Prophet Muhammad, peace and blessings be upon him, there were numerous and large differences among the communities and states of the world with regard to physical and spiritual attributes, abilities, and ways of life. For this reason, a single way of upbringing and a single invitation to the right path were not sufficient. Once that the world of humanity woke up with the sun of happiness of the time of Prophet Muhammad, peace and blessings be upon him, called the era of happiness, showed inclination towards unity, and started having communication and interaction by the exchange of ideas, the change and even abandoning of traditions, and the mixing of different tribes; and even the globe became like a single country, a single city, and even a single village; a single invitation to the right path and a single Prophethood appeared sufficient for all mankind.*"[226]

We are used to globalization in sports. The most globalized example in our globalizing world is probably football. Teams with more foreign players than nationals are not sneered at any more. Rather, the teams that can attract the best foreign stars receive high praise. At the end, all success, fame, and all kinds of gain belong to the team and the team's nation—no matter what the nationalities of the players and the coaches are. This became clear in the opening game of 2002 World Cup between France and Senegal. All eleven players of the Senegal national team were players in French teams, while all but one player in the French national team were players in the Italian and British teams, and seven of them were black. Furthermore, some the trainers of the national teams were of other nationalities.

This is also the case in science and learning. Sciences do not have nationalities. Scientists, who are like trees bearing the fruits of knowl-

---

[226] *İşârâtü'l-İ'câz*, p. 50.

edge, are judged on the basis of their scholarship and contribution to science, not their nationality. Scientists provide the greatest benefit to the company they work for, and to the country they live in. Companies and countries that can attract such people have a great advantage in this age of information. For instance, more than half of those who established the companies in the Silicon Valley, which has become a prominent center of the production of new technology, are people who immigrated to the USA. A football team that cannot transfer any foreign stars and loses its best players to foreign teams cannot be successful at national and international tournaments. Likewise, a country that cannot attract scholars from outside the country, and even worse, cannot keep its best minds and loses them to other countries, cannot be successful, and is certain to become a backward country. Even today, the existence of nations that dwell on racial superiority and turn its nose up at others, and look into its nationality as their source of strength rather than the sciences show that lessons are not learned from history. Those who turn away from science, reason, and knowledge, and bring forth national pride (in fact, their short sightedness and self-interest under this cover) are, knowingly or unknowingly, committing the worst act against that nation—destroying national pride and leading the nation into a humiliating backwardness.

The world economy has been largely globalized, and continues to be even more so at a fast pace. Customs are being lowered or eliminated by treaties, and the national borders have only a symbolic value for the entry and exit of goods and services. As a result, people who had to purchase goods produced in their country surrounded by the walls of customs, can now choose among goods produced in various countries in the world. Because of competition, local firms must either modernize and raise quality while lowering prices, or disappear from the marketplace. As a result of this worldwide market and the desire to have an edge, technology advances at a high pace, people can buy much higher quality goods at much lower prices, and the standard of living rises. All of humanity benefits from a globalized economy provided that it is equipped with measures against abusive practices such as monopoly and unfair competition.

Every animal can view the world as his personal property, with other animals serving as lively decorations and enrichment. A fish, for example, can view the ocean as his private aquarium. Animals are free to choose what to do, where to live, and when and where to migrate. Other than for food, they do not have to quarrel with each other. Therefore, we can say that animals benefit from all bounties of the world; and thus they are already as globalized as they can be.

However, the situation is different for mankind. Physically, a person is like a weak animal. But he has such vast senses, deep desires, and other faculties that the whole globe is like a ball in his hands. Like the desire of eternity, he has feelings that cannot be satisfied even if the whole world is given to him. As it is not possible to treat a patient before fully diagnosing and understanding his illness, so too it is not possible to write a prescription of joy for man before knowing the general nature of humankind. To get the most benefit from globalization while avoiding its potential dangers, it is essential to understand the nature of man. After all, both the globe and globalization are for humankind.

People live in a series of concentric social circles. The smallest circle of a person after his personal one is the family; the next one is the neighborhood he lives in, then the city, then the country, and finally the globe. Individuals have different roles and responsibilities in each circle, and the biggest responsibility is in the smallest circle. Being part of a city is not a threat to a family, and it does not require dissolving the family unit. In fact, the city provides support to family and its preservation and progress. Without a city, having roads and utilities such as water, electricity, natural gas, telephone, and sewer lines connected to our homes would be impossible for most people. The semi-civilized people who move their families outside the city limits to avoid the city rules, which are for the general well-being and safety of the city inhabitants, by viewing them as limitations on personal freedom, win little but lose a lot. Besides, a well-founded city government does not weaken the family structure; on the contrary, it strengthens the family structure.

Similar things can also be said for marriage, which can be viewed as 'globalization at the smallest level.' With marriage, many freedoms of single life are lost, and new responsibilities are assumed. But by becoming part of larger globe, the married individuals are now bigger, not smaller, and they are candidates for much bigger duties and rewards so long as they preserve their identity with mutual love and respect, and have common goals for the family unit. Families are building blocks of communities, and as such they have a share in every accomplishment of the community and its rewards. Despite some advantages of single life, and some marriages failing and ending in divorce, it is remarkable that a great majority of people takes the first step towards globalization with marriage.

Globalization is not the process of stripping every one of his or her identity and character, and creating individuals of a single type. Such a change would result in denial and rejection. In the words of Nursi, *"Mutual resemblance (similarity) is the cause of contradiction; congruity (being harmonious) is the basis of solidarity."*[227]

The concept of globalization is also applicable for inanimate beings. If it were not for globalization, the universe would not exist; and even if it did, it would be just a pile of dust. The fundamental building block of matter is the invisible neutrino particle, which is essentially a wave of energy and fills the entire universe and subatomic particles like the Higgs boson, which we have tried to observe. The electrons, protons, and neutrons that are made of neutrinos form the atom by arranging themselves in an orderly manner; the atoms combine to form molecules, molecules gather to make up parts, and the parts assemble to form meaningful items.

If hydrogen and oxygen atoms did not combine by sacrificing a little from their independence, there would be no water, no life, and probably no human beings. Hydrogen and oxygen did not lose anything from their core identity preserved in their nuclei by becoming part of a larger globe—water, for example, can easily separate into hydrogen and oxygen. But they have risen to the levels of 'wonderful' and 'glorious,' and formed the basis for the start of material life on earth. So by combining, they qualified for very high duties, and acquired very high positions and honors. If hydrogen and oxygen insisted on their indepen-

---

[227] *Sünûhât*, p. 56.

dence and remained as single atoms, they would remain as little insignificant spheres moving around aimlessly. If the atoms possessed consciousness, the self-centered, narrow-minded, and ignorant ones would object to losing part of their independence and having to be with foreign atoms at all times. Only broad-minded atoms with high aims would show the desire for globalization.

As the hydrogen and oxygen form water by globalizing, they form bonds only with their electrons on their outer orbit, and they do not lose anything from their core identity preserved in their nuclei. This is a must for a meaningful and harmonious unity. Otherwise, if we split the hydrogen and oxygen atoms and attempt to force the resulting particles and energy to unify, we will have a cloud of dust in our bucket instead of water.

Accomplishing major tasks and enjoying the resulting major fruits requires the existence of major globes. Therefore, the inter-planet (and even inter-galaxy) adventures that we see in space movies can only be possible after planet Earth is truly globalized. Otherwise, a planet that is too busy with internal bickering and fights between its member communities and unable to raise its head up cannot show a real existence in the galaxy. If the world can truly globalize and turn its attention to outer space, the resulting honor, dignity, and benefits will belong to all humanity—just like the whole of humanity landing on the moon in the persons of a few fellow human beings in 1960s, and every person feeling like having landed on the moon himself, and sharing the joy and honor.

The universe and humanity change constantly, and will continue changing. Those who turn their backs to the winds of change and try to preserve the current status are certain to become fossils among the pages of time. The question is not to change or not to change, it is how to change and to what to change. The speed and the direction of the winds of change play a major role in this decision. One cannot reach anywhere by rowing against the strong and continuous currents. As Nursi puts it, *"One should not oppose the general flow of events in a society. If he does, he will stumble and remain under the rubble."*[228]

---

[228] *İşârâtü'l-İ'câz*, p. 112.

Chapter 11

Positive and Negative Globalization

The sentiment that lies beneath the concerns associated with globalization is the fear that the strong will suppress the weak, the poor will get even poorer, and only the rich will collect the fruits of globalization. This is because it is difficult for the weak and the poor to defend their rights and freedoms against the strong and the wealthy. The past experience that the strong are always right increases this concern.

The greatest assurance against this concern is belief, spiritual advancement, and accepting that strength is in being right. As Bediüzzaman Said Nursi expresses it, *"Yes, just as the virtue arising from belief cannot be the means of oppression, so too it cannot be the cause of despotism. Oppression and arbitrary despotism indicate the absence of virtue. And the most important way of the people of virtue is to get involved in social life through impotence, poverty, and humility."*[229]

Dosage and the Balance between Benefit and Harm

Many things are being said and written for, or against, globalization. Some see globalization as a natural outcome of advancement and a new stage of civilization while others introduce globalization as a modern torturing machine that the strong will use to suppress the weak. Such differing views confuse people, and slow down the phase of globalization.

---

[229] Nursi, B. S., *The Flashes*, The Twenty-Second Flash, p. 227 (translation by Ş. Vahide), accessed September 29, 2014, www.dur.ac.uk/resources/sgia/imeis/3Fl09157-253.pdf.

The thing that should be known here is that "the difference between medicine and poison is its dosage." That is, a chemical that cures many people and illnesses can function like a poison if used in the wrong dosage or situation, and can cause even death. As it is wrong to introduce such a chemical as 'healer' without mentioning any limitations, and this would be invitation to abuse, it is just as wrong to oppose such a chemical totally because of its potential dangers when used incorrectly, as this would mean being without its benefits. The proper thing to do here is to approach the matter with good will, and to study this chemical scientifically, and to determine how to use this chemical in a beneficial way while avoiding its potential harms. Many people suffered from fire and knives, but no one suggested that we should stop using them. "*A lesser evil is acceptable for a greater good. If an evil which will lead to a greater good is abandoned so that a lesser evil should not occur, a greater evil will have been perpetrated.*"[230]

A major obstacle in major projects of great benefit is the stirring up of unfounded fears, unfair criticism, and dwelling on the negatives while ignoring the positives. In Nursi's words, "*And on important matters, he deceives and is deceived by his wiliness (one-sided deceptive view) that sees faults only. The result of this wiliness is to blow the faults out of proportion and to overshadow the good.*" "*The strange nature of this wiliness is to pull together the things scattered over time and place as one, and to view everything on that black screen.*"[231] "*Our worst mishap and sickness is that criticism which is based on pride and deception. If fairness utilizes criticism, it pares the truth. Whereas if it is pride that employs it, it mutilates and destroys it.*"[232]

"*A boat carrying numerous innocent people may not be sunk on account of one criminal. Similarly, enmity should not be nurtured towards a believer who possesses numerous innocent attributes, because of a single criminal attribute.*"[233] Similarly, to oppose globalization and all of

[230] Nursi, B. S., *The Letters*, The Twelfth Letter, p. 59 (translation by Ş. Vahide), accessed September 29, 2014, www.dur.ac.uk/resources/sgia/imeis/Lets1-13.pdf.
[231] *Münâzarât*, p. 34.
[232] *Hutbe-i Şâmiye*, p. 75.
[233] *Hutbe-i Şâmiye*, p. 144.

its major potential benefits because of some probable harm is a greater harm.

Nursi encourages us to attempt good works, and cautions against being overly suspicious:

"We should not be paranoid."[234]

"One of the most important and fundamental emotions in man is the sense of fear. Deceptive oppressors profit greatly from the vein of fear. They restrain the fearful with it." "They make people sacrifice most important things through most unimportant fears. Thinking that they are escaping from a mosquito bite, they flee into the dragon's mouth." "Almighty God gave the sense of fear to preserve life, not to destroy it! He did not give life so that it would be burdensome, difficult, painful, and torment. If fear is caused by a possibility of one in two, three, or four, or even one in five or six, it is a precautionary fear and may be licit. But to fear a possibility of one in twenty, thirty, or forty, is groundless, and makes life torture!"[235]

Strength in Unity

Unity is to the benefit of all. The greatest shared benefits arise from the biggest unifications. Being a form of unity, globalization can be the base for great projects and benefits. In the words of Nursi, *"The strength that is in a group does not exist in a person. For example, the strength in a rope that is formed by many strings, no longer exists when the strings are pulled apart."*[236]

"It is evident that if two champions are wrestling with each other, even a child can beat them. If two mountains are balanced in the scales, even a small stone can disturb their equilibrium and cause one to rise and the other to fall. O people of belief! Your strength is reduced to noth-

---

[234] *Sünûhât*, p. 36.

[235] Nursi, B. S., *The Letters*, The Twenty-Ninth Letter, p. 478 (translation by Ş. Vahide), accessed September 29, 2014, www.dur.ac.uk/resources/sgia/imeis/Lets29_2_SofR.pdf.

[236] *İşârâtü'l-İ'câz*, p. 107.

ing as a result of your passions and biased partisanships, and you can be defeated by the slightest forces."[237]

"A person sometimes loses what is good while seeking what is better. It is my contention that oftentimes good is better than what is better since there is unanimity concerning good but conflict concerning what is better. While searching for the better, there is permission for existence of falsehood. That is, sometimes pretty is prettier than the prettier."[238]

"The reason for the harmful conflict is to follow the rule 'it is the only right way' instead of the rule 'it is right'; and to subscribe to the rule 'it is the only good' instead of 'it is the best.' Instead of the merciful rule 'to love for the sake of Allah' the following rule was established 'to hate for the sake of Allah.' His dealings are dominated by the hatred towards other professions rather than the love of his own. The love for the truth is interfered by the siding with the ego. The means and evidences are situated in place of aims and goals.[239]

Nursi interprets the hadith 'Difference among my people is an instance of Divine Mercy' as follows: "*The difference intended in the hadith is a positive difference. That is, each party strives to promote and diffuse its own belief; it does not seek to tear down and destroy that of the other, but rather to improve and reform it. Negative difference is rejected by the hadith, for it aims in partisan and hostile fashion at mutual destruction, and those who are at each other's throats cannot act positively.*" "*If the confrontation of views takes place in the name of justice and for the sake of truth, then the difference concerns only means; there is unity with respect to aim and basic purpose. Such a difference makes manifest every aspect of the truth and serves justice and truth. But what emerges from a confrontation of views that is partisan and biased, and takes place for the sake of a tyrannical, evil-commanding soul, that is based on egotism and fame-seeking-what emerges from this is not the 'flash of truth,' but the fire of dissension.*"[240]

---

[237] *Mektubat*, pp. 305–306.
[238] *Sünûhât*, p. 89.
[239] Ibid., p. 74.
[240] *Mektubat*, pp. 303–304.

"However, unity cannot be established with ignorance. Unity is the unanimity of ideas. The unanimity of ideas can only be established with the light of electricity stemming from knowledge."[241]

Nature of Man

A real source of concern associated with globalization is the materialistic view of Western philosophy towards human beings. In this view, the human being is characterized as being a 'speaking animal,' 'economical animal,' and 'thinking animal.' The purpose of life is presented to be to satisfy the physical needs and desires like animals and to live in comfort; the righteousness is said to be in strength, and life is viewed as a constant struggle between interest groups. This approach has shaken the trust and safety among people, and brought forward the feelings of competition, animosity, and fear. The humanity paid a heavy price for this approach with two world wars.

Nursi has analyzed human beings by considering their physical as well as spiritual sides, and has pointed out that the true happiness of mankind is not in material things, but rather in virtue commensurate with his high nature. Pointing out that there is no limit in virtue and no need to compete for it, he showed mankind how to rise to new highs and how to find true happiness without fights:

"If judged by appearance only, a human being is like a tiny particle. But if attention is turned to the soul a human being possesses, the mind he carries in the head, and the capabilities he nurtures in his heart, the whole universe becomes small and cannot contain it. Yet the place that will satisfy the aspirations of the spirit, the ideas of the mind, and the tendencies of the capabilities is only the hereafter."[242]

"Although human beings are physically small, weak, and inept, and are considered to be from among animal species, they carry a very high soul, have great abilities, tendencies which cannot be bounded, endless aspirations, innumerable ideas, and unbounded senses such as lust and

---

[241] *Münâzarât*, p. 72.
[242] *İşârâtü'l-İ'câz*, p. 102.

wrath. And human beings have such a peculiar nature that as if they are created as an index to all species and worlds."[243]

"And also, the pleasures that a human being gets from physical animalistic life falls short of that a sparrow gets. For, a human being is inflicted with grief, sorrow, and fear whereas a sparrow is not. On the other hand, a human being can get greater pleasure than the greatest of the animals in regard to faculties, emotions, senses, and abilities one has."[244]

Feelings like oppression, greed, fear, and selfishness, and the ability of man to commit good and evil acts are limitless. Gathering widespread support for globalization and making it a reality depends on demonstrating that the true interest, safety, and advancement of all man are under the roof of globalization:

"Even if the whole world is given to man, with his greed, he will say: 'Are there any more?' And through his selfishness, he finds it acceptable that a thousand people should suffer harm for his own benefit. And so on. There is boundless development in bad morality and he may reach the degree of the Nimrods and Pharaohs; in accordance with the intensive form in the verse above, he is given to great wrongdoing. Similarly, he may manifest endless progress in good morality, and may advance to the degree of the Prophets and veracious ones."[245]

"Yes, human beings are created as adorers of themselves. In fact, a human being does not love anything more than he loves himself. He praises himself with words better suited for praising God. He defends himself zealously—whether he is right or wrong—by portraying himself above and beyond any fault or disgrace."[246]

"His desires extending to eternity, his thoughts that embrace all of creation and his wishes that embrace the different varieties of eternal bliss—that demonstrates he has been created for eternity and will indeed

---

[243] Ibid., p. 86.

[244] *Mesnevî-i Nuriye*, p. 206.

[245] Nursi, B. S., *The Letters*, The Twenty-Sixth Letter, p. 383 (translation by Ş. Vahide), accessed September 29, 2014, www.dur.ac.uk/resources/sgia/imeis/Lets24-26.pdf.

[246] *Mesnevî-i Nuriye*, p. 192.

proceed to eternity. This world is like a hospice for him, a waiting-room for the hereafter."[247]

"*If the jewel of true religion is not present in the shell of the heart, material, moral, and spiritual calamities of untold magnitude will break loose over mankind and they will become the most unhappy, the most wretched of animals.*"[248]

Planet Earth is the only globe we have, but there are as many interwoven personal globes as the number of people on earth. It can even be said that positive globalization is the process of establishing compatibility, support, and unity among these personal globes, and preventing any rejection and harm. In the words of Nursi, "*Moreover, everyone has his own vast world within this world. Simply, there are worlds one within the other to the number of human beings. The pillar of each person's private world is his own life. If his body gives way, his world collapses on his head, it is doomsday for him.*"[249]

However, the private worlds are the reflections of the real world on the mirrors of individuals, and these reflections take their color and shape from the mirrors, and thus from the nature and points of view of individuals. The universal globe can be said to be the combination of these personal globes. As Nursi puts is, "*Yes, everyone is limited by what is seen on his mirror. So it appears that your black and deceptive mirror has shown everything that way.*"[250] "*One picks the fruit that he likes and suits him well.*"[251]

---

[247] Nursi, B. S., *The Words*, The Tenth Word, p. 101 (translation by Ş. Vahide), accessed September 29, 2014, www.dur.ac.uk/resources/sgia/imeis/10thWord07.pdf.

[248] *Hutbe-i Şâmiye*, p. 22.

[249] Nursi, B. S., *The Flashes*, The Twenty-Sixth Flash, p. 297 (translation by Ş. Vahide), accessed September 29, 2014, www.dur.ac.uk/resources/sgia/imeis/4Fl09254-336.pdf.

[250] *Münâzarât*, p. 45.

[251] *Sünûhât*, p. 76.

Chapter 12

Principles of Positive Globalization

Mutual Assistance: The Most Important Bridge for the Maintenance of Humankind

N ursi sees mutual assistance as the key for peace and tranquility for people and classes of people. A healthy globalization can occur only if the channels of assistance to the less fortunate are kept wide open.

"*The bridge that maintains peace and order in social life is zakah [alms giving]. In humanity, the life of social life is born out of mutual assistance. The cure and remedy for the calamities that stem from uprisings, revolts, and conflicts that prevent the advancement of mankind is mutual assistance.*

"*There is great wisdom, a high benefit, and a vast mercy in implementing zakah and in forbidding usury. Yes, if you examine the page of the world from a historical perspective, and pay attention to the acts and faults that stain that page, you will see that all the uprisings, disorders, struggles, confrontations, and immorality are born out of two sayings: The first: So long as I am full, what is it to me if others die of hunger? And the second: you suffer hardship so that I can live in comfort with bounties and pleasures.*

"*It is only zakah that nulls and voids the first saying that brings the world of humanity to the verge of collapse by subjecting it to social earthquakes. And it is the prohibition of usury and interest that cuts the roots of the second saying that subjects the whole humanity to general col-*

lapse and destroys the peace and advancement by pushing people to bolshevism (communism).

"Friend! The biggest condition for maintaining order that protects the life of social life is to make sure that there are no gaps between classes. The distance between the upper classmen and the common people, and between the wealthy and the poor should not widen to the point that the relations between them are cut. The things that maintain communication between these classes are zakah and mutual assistance. However, the tension between these classes rise, lines of communications close, and visits and care among relatives disappears for not following the principles of prohibiting interest and implementing zakah. As a result, there will rise blasts of rebellion, shouts of rancor, and sounds of hatred and jealousy from the lower class towards the upper class in place of respect, obedience, and love. And the upper classes will descend on the common people with fires of cruelty, oppression, and lightning of humiliation in place of compassion, generosity, and kindness. It is unfortunate that while being a cause for modesty and compassion, the qualities of upper class are becoming causes for pride and arrogance. While being a cause for attracting compassion and generosity, the qualities of the lower class are resulting in slavery and poverty. If you want a witness for the things I have said, look at the civilized world—there are enough witnesses.

In summary, establishing peace between classes and maintaining relations and communication is possibly only by establishing zakah and its children charity and alms giving, which are among the pillars of Islam, as fundamental principles in social life."[252]

Cooperation: An Efficient Way to Meet the Endless Needs of People

Human beings must live together in communities and must cooperate, since their desires and needs are limitless, but their capabilities, resources, and time are limited. Otherwise, human beings cannot rise above the level of a weak animal that can hardly manage to feed itself. To live with dignity commensurate with being a human being, advancing in

---

[252] *İşârâtü'l-İ'câz*, pp. 44–45.

civilization, and to be the master of the planet and all the creatures living on it can only be possible by living together in communities and cooperating. The bigger and the more harmonious the community is, the bigger and sweeter the fruits of it will be. As Nursi puts it,

"Man is created, in a distinct and exceptional manner from all animals, with a peculiar and pleasant character. Because of this character, there appeared many kinds of tendencies and desires. For example, a human being wants the most distinctive things, inclines towards the most beautiful, desires the elegant things, and aspires to live in bounty with dignity commensurate with being a human.

"Man needs numerous crafts in order to meet his needs for food, clothing, and other needs, as these tendencies necessitate. As he does not possess mastery of those crafts, he is obliged to collaborate with his fellow human beings so that each person can help others by exchanging the goods and services produced, and this way they can meet their needs."[253]

"The worldly people, and even certain politicians and secret societies and manipulators of society, have taken as their guide the principle of shared property (incorporation) in order to obtain great wealth and power. They acquire an extraordinary strength and advantage, despite all their exploitation and harm. However, the nature of common property does not change with sharing, despite its many harms. Although each partner is as though the owner and supervisor of the rest in one respect, he cannot profit from this. Nevertheless, if this principle of shared property is applied to works pertaining to the Hereafter, it accumulates vast benefits, which produce no loss. For it means that all the property passes to the hands of each partner. For example, there are four or five men. With the idea of sharing, one of them brings paraffin, another a wick, another the lamp, another the mantle, and the fifth matches; they assemble the lamp and light it. Each of them becomes the owner of a complete lamp. If each of those partners has a full-length mirror on a wall, he will be reflected in it together with the lamp and room, without deficiency or being split up."[254]

---

[253] Ibid., p. 84.
[254] Nursi, B. S., *The Flashes*, The Twenty-First Flash, p. 219 (translation by Ş. Vahide), accessed September 29, 2014, www.dur.ac.uk/resources/sgia/imeis/3Fl09157-253.pdf.

"Craftsmen are acquiring significant wealth through cooperating in order to profit more from the products of their crafts. Formerly ten men who made sewing needles all worked on their own, and the fruit of their individual labor were three needles a day. Then in accordance with the rule of joint enterprise the ten men united. One brought the iron, one lit the furnace, one pierced the needles, one placed them in the furnace, and another sharpened the points, and so on . . . each was occupied with only part of the process of the craft of needle-making. Since the work in which he was employed was simple, time was not wasted, he gained skill, and performed the work with considerable speed. Then they divided up the work which had been in accordance with the rule of joint enterprise and the division of labor: they saw that instead of three needles a day, it worked out at three hundred for each man. This event was widely published among the craftsmen of 'the worldly' in order to encourage them to pool their labor."[255]

If it is this way in material things that decrease with sharing, it will be even more magnificent for nonmaterial things such as love and compassion that increase with sharing, and the amount of happiness per individual will increase as happiness spreads.

Justice: Absolute Equality before Law

Preserving order in societies and preventing animosity can only happen by upholding justice, and the first requirement for a healthy globalization is the establishment of global justice. In the words of Nursi,

"Equality is not in honor and virtue—it is before law. A king and a slave are equal before law. Curiously, if a Divine law cautions against knowingly stepping on ants, restrains from tormenting them, how can it neglect the rights of human beings? Never . . . We did not conform to this rule. Yes, the trial of Ali with an ordinary Jew, and our pride Salahaddin Ayyubi's court challenge with an ordinary Christian, should correct your misunderstanding, I believe."[256]

---

[255] Ibid., p. 220.
[256] *Münâzarât*, p. 30.

Nursi views belief as the guarantee to prevent injustice, and as the guardian of freedom:

"Belief necessitates not humiliating others through oppression and despotism and not degrading them, and, secondly, not belittling oneself before tyrants."[257]

"For, a man who becomes a servant of the Master of Universe by embracing faith, his self-respect and heroism of faith will never let him lower himself before others, and accept to serve under the rule of an oppressor. Likewise, the compassion that stems from his faith will not allow him to violate the rights and freedoms of others. Yes, a righteous servant of a Sultan will not lower himself as to accept the dominance of a shepherd. That servant will also hold himself above dominating a helpless person. So the more perfect the faith is, the brighter the sun of freedom shines. Here is the time of Prophet Muhammad (referred to as the Age of Happiness)."[258]

Justice: Being Just While Evaluating Mistakes and Faults

The preservation of peace and tranquility in a society depends on being fair and the first condition of establishing peace in the world is establishing global justice:

"A satanic wile corrupting the life of society is this: not to see all the virtues of a believer on account of a single bad point. Those unjust people who heed this wile of Satan are in this way inimical to believers. However, when Almighty God weighs up deeds with absolute justice on the supreme scales at the Last Judgment, He will judge in accordance with the predominance of good deeds over evils and vice versa. Seeing that the causes of evil deeds are numerous and their existence is easy, sometimes He veils numerous bad deeds with a single good deed. That is to say, dealings in this world should be in accordance with Divine justice. If a person's good points are greater in regard to quality or quantity than his bad points, he is deserving of love and respect. Indeed, one should forgive numerous bad points on account of a single laudable virtue. How-

---

[257] *Hutbe-i Şâmiye*, p. 60.

[258] *Münâzarât*, p. 23.

ever, due to the vein of tyranny in his nature, at the promptings of Satan, the person forgets the hundred virtues of others because of a single bad point; he is hostile towards his believing brother, and commits sins. Just as a fly's wing covering the eye conceals a mountain, so too, the veil of hatred makes man conceal virtues as great as a mountain due to a single evil resembling a fly's wing; he forgets them, is hostile towards his brother believer, and becomes a tool of corruption in the life of society."[259]

It is difficult to have healthy globalization unless such positive and constructive approach in daily affairs is established.

Prejudice and Bigotry: Seeing Everything Black by Wearing Black Glasses

One of the biggest obstacles on the path of globalization is bigotry that narrows people's angle of view, and causes them to view everything with suspicion and enmity. The reason for bigotry is ignorance, and its remedy is enlightenment with knowledge. Nursi states that the obstacle of bigotry has largely disappeared with the advance of civilization: *"In this time of modern civilization, the Europeans are civilized and powerful, and harmful hostility and bigotry have therefore disappeared. For, in respect of religion, the civilized are to be conquered through persuasion, not through force, and through showing by conforming to its commands in actions and conduct that Islam is elevated and lovable. Force and enmity are only to combat the barbarity of savages."*[260]

The world has been changing face for a hundred years. Personal bigotry and ignorance are being replaced by common sense and knowledge, which are the common possessions of mankind. In the end, unity arises from the sharing of common values, and people are becoming more civilized. This civilization process will continue faster and disagreements will be settled by negotiating, not by force.

---

[259] Nursi, B. S., *The Flashes*, The Thirteenth Flash, p. 219 (translation by Ş. Vahide), accessed September 29, 2014, www.dur.ac.uk/resources/sgia/imeis/3Fl09157-253.pdf.

[260] *Hutbe-i Şâmiye*, s. 95.

Tranquility: The Treasure Earned by Keeping Rancor and Enmity out of the Heart

In this globalizing world, having lasting peace depends on the ending of animosities and the establishment of mutual assistance: *"If then you love yourself, do not permit this harmful hostility and desire for revenge to enter your heart. If it has entered your heart, do not listen to what it says. Hear what truth-seeing Hafiz of Shiraz says: 'The world is not a commodity worth arguing over.' It is worthless since it is transient and passing. If this is true of the world, then it is clear how worthless and insignificant are the petty affairs of the world! Hafiz also said: 'The tranquility of both worlds lies in the understanding of these two words: generosity towards friends, peaceful relations towards enemies.'"*[261]

Nursi warns people against greed, rancor, and envy that destroy peace and order in social life, and insists on establishing the practice of *zakah* (alms giving) to cure these social diseases effectively: *"Solidarity in a society results in harmony in all its activities, while mutual envy causes all its activities to come to a standstill."*[262]

"Humanity and Islam that necessitate love are like the Uhud Mountain. The causes that result in hostility are like small pebbles. The person who allows hostility to overcome love has behaved, in the sense of reality, with such stupidity as to lowering Uhud Mountain below the level of a pebble. Hostility and love, like darkness and light, cannot coexist. If hostility prevails, love turns to cordiality. If love prevails, hostility changes to compassion and pity. My path is to love love, and to be hostile to hostility. That is, the thing I love the best in the world is love, and the things I despise the most are hostility and enmity."[263]

These principles are applicable everywhere and for all in this globalizing world.

---

[261] *Mektubat*, p. 302.
[262] Nursi, B. S., *The Letters*, Seeds of Reality, p. 536 (translation by Ş. Vahide), accessed September 29, 2014, www.dur.ac.uk/resources/sgia/imeis/Lets29_2_SofR.pdf.
[263] *Münâzarât*, p. 77.

Love, Virtue, and Generosity:
Basic Building Blocks of Social Life

Nursi attracts attention to the positive attributes engraved on the basic human nature such as love, perfection, and generosity, and expresses these attributes that can serve as the basic building blocks for globalization as follows:

"The first steps to the perfection and enhancement of social structure are brotherhood and love."[264]

"Included in human nature are a love of beauty, an ardor for perfection, and passion for bestowal. His love increases proportionately to the degrees of beauty, perfection, and bestowal, reaching the furthest degrees of ecstatic ardor . . . It is clear that just as man takes pleasure at his own happiness, so he receives pleasure at the happiness of others to whom he is attached. And just as he loves someone who saves him from disaster, so he loves someone who saves those he loves."[265]

"It is well known that the most indisputable virtue is the one that is testified and affirmed even by one's enemies."[266]

Nursi sees responding to evil with good as the prescription for curing hatred and enmity, and enhancing love: *"If you wish to defeat your enemy, then respond to his evil with good. For if you respond with evil, enmity will increase, and even though he will be outwardly defeated, he will nurture hatred in his heart, and hostility will persist. . . . It often happens that if you tell an evil man, 'You are good, you are good,' he will become good; and if you tell a good man, 'You are bad, you are bad,' he will become bad."*[267]

"Civilization necessitates affection and love for humanity."[268]

---

[264] *İşârâtü'l-İ'câz*, p. 86.

[265] Nursi, B. S., *The Flashes*, The Eleventh Flash, p. 91 (translation by Ş. Vahide), accessed September 29, 2014, www.dur.ac.uk/resources/sgia/imeis/2Fl0981-156.pdf.

[266] *Hutbe-i Şâmiye*, p. 94.

[267] *Mektubat*, p. 300.

[268] *Münâzarât*, p. 27.

Consultation: The Key for Advancement, Efficiency, and Tranquility

Nursi views consultation as the engine for the advancement of mankind and civilization and as the source of happiness, and strongly recommends spreading the practice of consultation at all levels:

"Because just consultation results in sincerity and solidarity, three 'ones' become one hundred and eleven. Thus, three men between whom there is true solidarity may benefit the nation as much as a hundred men. Many historical events inform us that as a result of true sincerity, solidarity, and consultation, ten men may perform the work of a thousand men."[269]

"The key to Muslims' happiness in Islamic social life is the mutual consultation enjoined by the Sharia. The verse, 'Whose rule is consultation among themselves [Qur'an 42:38]' orders consultation as a fundamental principle. Just as the consultation of the ages and centuries that mankind has practiced by means of history, a conjunction of ideas, formed the basis of the progress and sciences of all mankind, so too one reason for the backwardness of Asia, the largest continent, was the failure to practice that true consultation."[270]

Belief: A Source of Brotherhood and Love

Another dimension of globalization is the unity formed by the ties of belief. With the verse *'All believers are only brothers* (al-Hujurat-10),' Qur'an expresses that all believers form a globe in which believers are connected to each other with the ties of brotherhood. Nursi expresses this as follows:

"Yes, like a believing person viewing the universe as a place of brotherhood as required by belief in God and its oneness, the rope that interconnects all creation, especially human beings, in particular Muslims, is only brotherhood. Because belief portrays all believers as brothers just like the brothers living under the protection of a compassionate father. But non-belief is such coldness that it turns even real brothers to strang-

---

[269] *Hutbe-i Şâmiye*, p. 60.
[270] Ibid.

ers. And it plants the seeds of isolation in all existence. And it makes every-thing the enemy of one another."[271]

"Belief establishes real brotherhood, connection, unification, and solidarity among all things. But non-belief, like chill, exhibits all things as unrelated to one another, and portrays them as strangers to one anoth-er. For this reason, there is no enmity, hostility, and violence in the spir-it of a believer. He has some level of brotherhood even with his greatest enemy. But a non-believer has greed and enmity in his spirit, as well as having confidence in himself and counting on himself."[272]

"Thus, through the bond of this sacred nationhood, all the people of Islam are like a single tribe. Like the members of a tribe, the groups of Islam are bound and connected to one another through Islamic brother-hood. They assist one another morally and, if necessary, materially. It is as if all the groups of Islam are bound to each other with a luminous chain."[273]

"The difference between the civilization of unbelievers and the civi-lization of believers: the first is scary brutality wearing the dress of civi-lization. Its outside shines, but the inside burns. Its outside is glitz, but the inside is filth; it is a devil whose exterior is lovely, but the interior is the opposite. The second is light inside and compassion outside. It is mercy outside and brotherhood inside; it is a fascinating angel whose exterior is mutual assistance and the interior is compassion."[274]

Eliminating the concern for injustice is only possible by establish-ing that strength in righteousness—not the reverse. This can be done by enforcing fair rules that conform to general wisdom and human conscience. Using such rules as the base in human affairs provides gen-eral peace and order in a society, and satisfies the sense of justice. This, in turn, increases the enthusiasm and passion, which is the key for advancement, and eliminates hopelessness, which is the biggest obsta-cle to advancement. In the words of Nursi:

---

[271] *Mesnevî-i Nuriye*, p. 79.

[272] Ibid., pp. 60–61.

[273] *Hutbe-i Şâmiye*, p. 53.

[274] *Mesnevî-i Nuriye*, p. 79.

"However, injustices and aggressions occur in human affairs since the power of passion (animal appetite), the power of anger (madness), and the power of reason (intelligence) in human beings are not limited by the Creator, and these powers are set free to provide the advancement of man. To prevent these aggressions, the world community needs justice in exchanging the fruits of their work. But the mind of individuals is far from comprehending justice, and thus there is a need for a comprehensive mind so that individuals benefit from that comprehensive mind. Such a comprehensive mind can be only in the form of law."[275]

---

[275] *İşârâtü'l-İ'câz*, p. 85.

Chapter 13

Globalization and Nationalism

G lobalization is often thought to be a rival to nationalism, and is perceived to be a threat to the existence of nations. For this reason, often there is rivalry between the nationalists and the supporters of globalization. But globalization is not a threat to nationalism; to the contrary, globalization can serve as a protective envelope for different nationalities.

Globalization does not require the denial of nations, and the lifting of national borders. To the contrary, it can provide the proper environment for the nations to preserve their identity and existence and to develop healthily in peace and solidarity. It can prevent the animosity and confrontations that can result in the vanishing of some nations. The efforts of United Nations, NATO, and the European Union in this regard are well known.

The social circles of family, city, and nation are necessary for people to provide support to each other, and the lifting of those circles may cause chaos and inefficiency. An army that gets rid of its units such as divisions, regiments, battalions, and squads loses its effectiveness and power to a great extent. As it is unthinkable for a military to get rid of its structural units, it is also unthinkable to disregard national borders and to ignore the presence of different nations on earth.

The Qur'an explains the merits of being created as different nations and cautions us against the abuse of this differentiation as follows: "*O mankind! We created you from a single pair of a male and a female, and made you into nations and tribes, that you may know each other*" (al-

Hujurat 49:13). Nursi interprets this verse in the 3rd Section of "The Twenty-Sixth Letter" as follows: *"That is, 'I created you as peoples, nations, and tribes, so that you should know one another and the relations between you in social life, and assist one another; not so that you should regard each other as strangers, refusing to acknowledge one another, and nurturing hostility and enmity.'"*

And then he continues as follows: *"In order to explain the principle of 'knowing and assisting each other' which the verse indicates, we say this: An army is divided into divisions, the divisions into regiments, the regiments into battalions, companies, and then into squads, so that every soldier may know his many different connections and their related duties; then the members of the army may truly perform a general duty governed by the principle of mutual assistance, and their social life be guarded against the attacks of the enemy. This arrangement is not so that divided and split up, one company should compete with another, one battalion be hostile to another, and one division act in opposition to another.*

"In just the same way, Islamic Society as a whole is a huge army, which has been divided into tribes and groups. But it has a thousand and one aspects of unity. Its groups' Creator is one and the same, their Provider is one and the same, their Prophet is one and the same, their qibla is one and the same, their Book is one and the same, their country is one and the same; all the same, a thousand things are one and the same.

"Thus, this many things being one and the same requires brotherhood, love, and unity. That is to say, being divided into groups and tribes is for mutual acquaintance and mutual assistance, not for antipathy and mutual hostility."[276]

For fellow citizens, nationalism can serve as a means of getting to know each other and providing support to each other. But when it is abused, it may become a headache for the humanity—as it happened during World War II. Instead of being for or against it, Nursi has analyzed nationalism, and showed how to take advantage of its benefits while avoiding its potential harms as follows:

---

[276] Nursi, B. S., *The Letters*, The Twenty-Sixth Letter, p. 372 (translation by Ş. Vahide), accessed September 29, 2014, www.dur.ac.uk/resources/sgia/imeis/Lets24-26.pdf.

"However, nationalism is of two kinds. One is negative, inauspicious, and harmful; it is nourished by devouring others, persists through hostility to others, and is aware of what it is doing. It is the cause of enmity and disturbance. It is because of this that the hadith states: 'Islam has abrogated what preceded it, and put an end to the Tribalism of the Ignorance State.'"[277]

"Also, the European nations have advanced the idea of racialism much this century; the ghastly events of the Great War showed how harmful for mankind is negative nationalism, as well as the perpetual and ill-omened enmity of the French and Germans."[278]

"Positive nationalism arises from an inner need of social life and is the cause of mutual assistance and solidarity; it ensures a beneficial strength; it is a means for further strengthening Islamic brotherhood."[279]

"To those people who go to excess in the idea of negative nationalism and racialism we say this:

"Firstly, the face of the world and especially this country of ours has since ancient times seen numerous migrations and changes of population. In addition, when the center of Islamic rule was established here other peoples were drawn to it and they settled here. Consequently, only when the Preserved Tablet is revealed will the races truly be distinguished from each other. To construct movements and patriotism on the idea of true race is both meaningless and extremely harmful. It is for this reason that one of the nationalist leaders and racialists, who was very neglectful in religion, was compelled to say: 'If language and religion are the same, the nation is the same.' Since that is so, what will be taken into consideration will be relations of language, religion, and country, not true race. If the three are the same, that certainly is a strong nation. And if one is absent, it is still within the bounds of nationalism."[280]

---

[277] Nursi, B. S., *The Letters*, The Twenty-Sixth Letter, p. 373 (translation by Ş. Vahide), accessed September 29, 2014, www.dur.ac.uk/resources/sgia/imeis/Lets24-26.pdf.

[278] Ibid.

[279] Ibid., p. 374.

[280] Ibid., p. 377.

"Like a soldier having a connection and a related duty in his squad, company, battalion, and division, everybody has a range of connections and related duties in social circles. If there was disarray with no inter-connections, there would be no meeting and assisting among people.

The awakening of racialism is either positive—comes to life with compassion towards others and is a cause of meeting and mutual assistance. Or it is negative—comes to life with racial bias and care and is a cause of enmity and denial of others. Islam rejects this."[281]

Nursi explains as follows that the time of racialism has passed, and that racialism cannot be taken as the basis for nations any longer: *"Perhaps the previous century could have been the age of nationalism. This century is not the age of racialism! Communism and socialism occupy all matters, destroying the idea of racialism. The age of racialism is passing."*[282] As a matter of fact, the European countries moved away from the idea of nationalism. However, some countries like Turkey could not read the time well and had to pay for their mistakes. The gap between South Korea, which read the values of time well, and North Korea, which broke off its relationships with time, shows an exemplary case. Nursi continues his warnings about racism as follows:

"Blind racialism is a blend made up of heedlessness, immorality, wickedness, hypocrisy, and darkness that support one another. For this reason, nationalists regard nationalism as something to be worshipped. But the Islamic zeal is a radiating light that reflects from the glow of belief."[283]

"Since the principles of racialism and nationalism do not follow justice and right, they are tyranny. They do not proceed on justice. For a ruler of racialist leanings prefers those of the same race, and cannot act justly."[284]

"For each nation, there is a virtual pool which constitutes the national self-esteem, protects the national self-respect, and houses the strength

---

[281] *Sünûhât*, p. 6.

[282] Nursi, B. S., *The Letters*, The Twenty-Ninth Letter, p. 503 (translation by Ş. Vahide), accessed September 29, 2014, www.dur.ac.uk/resources/sgia/imeis/Lets29_2_SofR.pdf.

[283] *Mesnevî-i Nuriye*, p. 102

[284] Nursi, B. S., *The Letters*, The Fifteenth Letter, p. 72 (translation by Ş. Vahide), accessed September 29, 2014, www.dur.ac.uk/resources/sgia/imeis/Lets15-18.pdf.

of that nation. There is also a virtual treasury, which constitutes the national wealth, provides general welfare, and houses the surplus goods . . .

"A man who does not have the sense of self-defense which is the power of anger, and the attraction which is the power of passion has essentially died, and is considered dead even if he is alive. A locomotive engine whose steam boiler has holes is in disarray and lacks the ability to move. The beads of a prayer bead whose string is broken scatter all around. Similarly, the heads that empty the treasury and the virtual pool housing the strength and goods of a nation cut the rope of nationalism, and turn it into pieces while they make members of that nation vagabond, devastated, and vanished."[285]

Thermodynamics and Globalization

Thermodynamics is the science of energy. The magnitude of a system can be represented by its "energy content," while its figure of merit by its work potential or "energy content." As humans, we tend to perceive bigger things as being better. But experience shows that often this is not the case, confirming the phrase, "bigger is not necessarily better." In the 1930s, Nursi expressed this as follows: *"If the community is not truly united as one, addition and unification makes smaller, like multiplying fractions. It is well known that in arithmetic that multiplication and addition increase: four times four makes sixteen. While in fractions, on the contrary, multiplication and addition make smaller: a third multiplied by a third makes a ninth. In just the same way, if there is not integral wholeness, common direction, and unity among people, they become smaller, impure, and worthless by multiplying."*[286]

Thermodynamic concepts and principles can be used to analyze merging and breaking-up processes in daily life, using energy destruction associated with various processes as a guide, with the following results:

---

[285] *Münâzarât*, pp. 54–57.
[286] Nursi, B. S., *The Letters*, Seeds of Reality, p. 536 (translation by Ş. Vahide), accessed September 29, 2014, www.dur.ac.uk/resources/sgia/imeis/Lets29_2_SofR.pdf.

Combining thermodynamic systems that are identical or almost identical will result in a larger system with a larger energy content, and thus uniting compatible things will result in a larger single item with a much larger figure of merit.

Combining two thermodynamic systems that are at different states yields a system that is larger in size, but smaller in energy content. To avoid waste of work potential, such systems should be operated separately. Uniting very different things will result in a larger single item, but with a much smaller figure of merit, and thus incompatible things should not be forced to be joined under one rule. Instead, they should be allowed to exist separately, and their outputs should be combined so that they support rather than cancel each other. Combining systems to form a single larger and more powerful system is good only if the individual systems work in harmony in the new larger unit, and thus there is little or no destruction of figure of merit. Items that are compatible in some aspects and incompatible in other aspects should be combined only partially, involving the compatible aspects only. The individual items should maintain their individuality in regard to the incompatible aspects.

These principles can be used as guiding light in globalization considerations as they shed light on the proper level of globalization. The world would be a better place to live if entropy generation and thus energy destruction are minimized. This can be done by eliminating all expenditures that add nothing to the quality of life. For example, a large fraction of state budgets is set aside for military expenses, and people spend years in mandatory military service. We are paying a heavy toll for the distrust among each other. Globalization that reduces or eliminates this distrust can add significantly to the quality of life for all. However, it is necessary to establish global security to do it.

Chapter 14

Mutual Assistance and Global View

Nursi sees mutual assistance as the key to peace and tranquility for people and classes of people. A healthy globalization can occur only if the channels of assistance to the less fortunate are kept wide open.

"*The bridge that maintains peace and order in social life is zakah (alms giving). In humanity, the life of social life is born out of mutual assistance. The cure and remedy for the calamities that stem from uprisings, revolts, and conflicts that prevent the advancement of mankind is mutual assistance.*"[287]

"*Zakah (alms giving) is a most essential pillar for happiness—not merely for individuals and particular societies, but for all of humanity. There are two classes of men: the upper classes and the common people. It is only zakah that will induce compassion and generosity in the upper classes toward the common people, and respect and obedience in the common people toward the upper classes. In the absence of zakah, the upper classes will descend on the common people with cruelty and oppression, and the common people will rise up against the upper classes in rancor and rebellion. There will be a constant struggle, a persistent opposition between the two classes of men. It will finally result in the confrontation of capital and labor, as happened in Russia.*"[288]

Eliminating the concern for injustices is only possible by establishing that strength is in righteousness—not the reverse. This can be

---

[287] *İşârâtü'l-İ'câz*, pp. 44–45.
[288] *Mektubat*, p. 310.

done by enforcing fair rules that conform to general wisdom and the human conscience. Using such rules as the base in human affairs provides general peace and order in a society, and satisfies the sense of justice. This, in turn, increases the enthusiasm and passion, which is the key for advancement, and eliminates hopelessness, which is the biggest obstacle to advancement. Nursi argues as follows that the foundations of world peace and tranquility cannot be laid by the current form of Western Civilization, and they need to be improved further:

"The Qur'an, which is a mercy for mankind, only accepts a civilization that comprises the happiness of all, or at least of the majority. Modern civilization has been founded on five negative principles:

- Its point of support is force, the mark of which is aggression.

- Its aim and goal is benefit, the mark of which is jostling and tussling.

- Its principle in life is conflict, the mark of which is strife.

- The bond between the masses is racialism and negative nationalism, which is nourished through devouring (gulping down) others; its mark is collision.

- Its enticing service is inciting lust and passion and gratifying the desires. But lust transforms man into a beast."[289]

Nursi describes a civilization that is based on Islam, is acceptable to all people, and can form the foundations of world peace and tranquility as follows:

"- Its point of support is truth instead of force, the mark of which is justice and harmony.

- Its goal is virtue in place of benefit, the mark of which is love and attraction.

- Its means of unity are the ties of religion, country, and class, in place of racialism and nationalism, and the mark of these is sincere brotherhood, peace, and only defense against external aggression.

- Its life is the principle of mutual assistance instead of the principle of conflict, the mark of which is accord and solidarity.

---

[289] Nursi, B. S., *The Letters*, Seeds of Reality, p. 535 (translation by Ş. Vahide), accessed September 29, 2014, www.dur.ac.uk/resources/sgia/imeis/Lets29_2_SofR.pdf.

- It is salvation instead of lust, the mark of which is human progress and spiritual advancement."[290]

"And the mark of 'the truth' is accord. The mark of virtue is 'solidarity.' The mark of mutual assistance is 'hastening to assist one another.' The mark of religion is 'brotherhood' and 'attraction.' And the mark of reining in and tethering the soul and leaving the spirit free and urging it towards perfections is 'happiness in this world and the one after."[291]

Nursi compares those who subscribe to materialist philosophy and the Islamic philosophy as follows:

"The student of philosophy runs away from his brother, and sues him. But the student of the Qur'an, viewing all obedient servants of God in the heavens and the earth as brothers, prays sincerely for their well-being, becomes happy with their happiness, and feels a deep connection in his soul towards them. Even though he does not view Heaven worthy of his worship and remembrance of God, he does not see himself as being above even the tiniest creature of God, combining extreme modesty with utmost dignity."[292]

"The pupil who has absorbed your instruction thoroughly becomes a pharaoh. But he is an abject pharaoh who worships the basest things and holds himself to be lord over everything he reckons advantageous. A student of yours is obstinate, but an obstinate wretch who accepts utter abasement for a single pleasure. *He is so despicable as to kiss Satan's foot for some worthless benefit. And he is a bully. But because he has nothing in his heart on which to rely, he is an impotent bullying braggart. His whole aim and endeavor is to satisfy the lusts of his soul, to cunningly seek his own personal interests under the screen of patriotism and devotion, and work to satisfy his ambition and pride. He loves seriously nothing at all other than himself and sacrifices everything for his own sake.*

---

[290] Nursi, B. S., *The Letters*, Seeds of Reality, p. 535 (translation by Ş. Vahide), accessed September 29, 2014, www.dur.ac.uk/resources/sgia/imeis/Lets29_2_SofR.pdf.

[291] Nursi, B. S., *The Words*, p. 146 (translation by Ş. Vahide), accessed September 29, 2014, www.dur.ac.uk/resources/sgia/imeis/words11-14_07_.pdf.

[292] *Mesnevî-i Nuriye*, p. 142.

"As for the sincere, wholehearted student of the Qur'an, he is a worshipping servant. But he is an esteemed servant who does not stoop to bow in worship before even the mightiest of creatures, and does not make the supreme benefit of Paradise the aim of his worship. And he is mild and gentle, but at the same time noble and gracious and lowers himself before none but the All-Glorious Creator, and only stoops before the lowly with His permission and at His command. And he is needy, but due to the reward his All-Generous Owner is storing up for him in the future, he is at the same time self-sufficient. And he is weak, but he is strong in his weakness for he relies on the strength of his Lord whose power is infinite. Would the Qur'an make its true student take this fleeting, transient world as his aim and purpose while not making him have even eternal Paradise as his goal? Thus, you can understand how different from one another are the aims and endeavors of the two students."[293]

A Bright Future

Although the potential benefits that technological innovations can offer to humanity are quite clear, most people view Western civilization with concern and suspicion. The reason is past experience: When power was gathered in the wrong hands, people still remember how it was used as an instrument to oppress the weak, and how it benefited a small minority while enslaving the majority, and how it caused devastation through wars because of greed. The real civilization that will bring happiness, wealth, and dignity to the whole humanity and make the world a wonderful place to live is only possible by refurbishing the current civilization with Islam which is based on justice, love, and virtue. Nursi gives the good news that such a civilization will develop from the development of current civilization. He also give the glad tidings that the 'real' civilization equipped with general peace and tranquility will rule in the future, and asks people to abandon pessimism and embrace hope:

"The religion of good and truth shall absolutely prevail in the future so that, as is the case with all other beings, good and virtue will prevail

---

[293] Nursi, B. S., *The Flashes*, The Seventeenth Flash, pp. 163–164 (translation by Ş. Vahide), accessed September 29, 2014, www.dur.ac.uk/resources/sgia/imeis/3Fl09157-253. pdf.

absolutely over mankind; and mankind may be equal to the rest of their brothers in the universe; and it may be said that the mystery of pre-eternal wisdom is established in mankind also."[294]

"Through civilization's iniquities and crimes prevailing over its benefits and its evils being preferred to its virtues, mankind has suffered two calamitous blows in the form of two world wars, and overturning that sinful civilization have been so utterly disgusted that they have smeared the face of the earth with blood. Insha'llah [God willing], through the strength of Islam in the future, the virtues of civilization will predominate, the face of the earth cleansed of filth, and universal peace be secured.

"Indeed, the facts that European civilization is not founded on virtue and guidance but rather on lust and passion, rivalry and oppression, and that up to the present the evils of civilization have predominated over its virtues, and that it has been infiltrated by revolutionary societies like a worm-eaten tree are each like powerful indications and means for the supremacy of Asian civilization. And in a short period of time it will prevail."

"Since the inclination to seek perfection has been included in man's essential nature, for sure, if doomsday does not soon engulf man as a result of his errors and tyranny, in the future truth and justice will show the way to a worldly happiness in the world of Islam, insha'llah, in which there will be atonement for the former errors of mankind."

"Just as every winter is followed by spring and every night by morning, mankind, also, shall have a morning and a spring, insha'llah. You may expect from Divine Mercy to see real civilization within universal peace brought about through the sun of the truth of Islam."[295]

"The truths of Islam will be the means of delivering man from the low and debased degree to which he has fallen, of cleansing the face of the earth, and securing universal peace. We beseech this from the mercy of the All-Merciful and Compassionate One, and we await it with hope."[296]

---

[294] *Hutbe-i Şâmiye*, p. 42.
[295] Ibid., pp. 36–38.
[296] Ibid., p. 43.

References

Nursi, Bediüzzaman Said, *Âsâr-ı Bediiyye*, (Compilation and Translation: Abdülkadir Badıllı), Elmas Neşriyat, İstanbul, 2004.

_____ *Dîvân-ı Harb-i Örfî*, Yeni Asya Neşriyat, İstanbul, 2011.

_____ *Emirdağ Lahikası*, Şahdamar Yayınları, İstanbul, 2012.

_____ *Hutbe-i Şâmiye*, Envar Neşriyat, İstanbul, 2012.

_____ *İşârâtü'l-İ'câz*, Şahdamar Yayınları, İstanbul, 2012.

_____ *Kastamonu Lahikası*, Şahdamar Yayınları, İstanbul, 2012.

_____ *Lem'alar*, Şahdamar Yayınları, İstanbul, 2012.

_____ *Mektubat*, Şahdamar Yayınları, İstanbul, 2012.

_____ *Mesnevi-i Nuriye*, Şahdamar Yayınları, İstanbul, 2012.

_____ *Muhakemât*, Şahdamar Yayınları, İstanbul, 2012.

_____ *Münâzarât*, Envar Neşriyat, İstanbul, 2012.

_____ *Sözler*, Şahdamar Yayınları, İstanbul, 2012.

_____ *Sünûhât*, Envar Neşriyat, İstanbul, 2012.

_____ *Şuâlar*, Şahdamar Yayınları, İstanbul, 2012.

_____ *Tarihçe-i Hayat*, Şahdamar Yayınları, İstanbul, 2012.